PLOUGH

YOUR

MIND

PLOUGH YOUR MIND

FINE TUNING YOUR BRAIN SYNTHESIZER

Dr. ANURUTI RAI

Title: PLOUGH YOUR MIND

Author: Dr. Anuruti Rai

First Edition

Copyright © 2022 Dr. Anuruti Rai

ISBN: 978-93-5602-934-7

Published by:

Dr. Anuruti Rai

E-mail: dentamedpublishing@gmail.com

Although every precaution has been taken in the preparation of this book, the publisher and author assume no responsibility for errors or omissions. Neither is any liability assumed for damages resulting from the use of this information contained herein.

DEDICATION

Dedicated to those who realize that the toughest war to win is against yourself, every single day and emerge victorious to yourself much before the world labels you successful.

Contents

PART II

4. Understanding your Mind Soil

5. Plough your mind

6. Uproot the weeds

7. Sow the seeds

8. Crop rotation

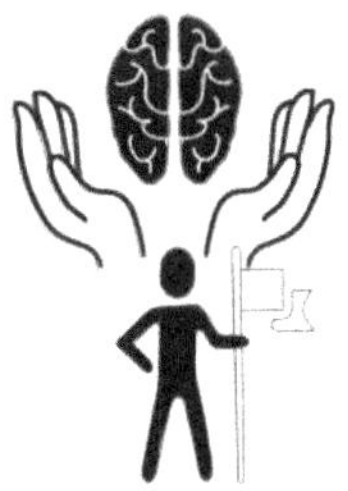

9. Conserve your mind soil

CONTENTS

PART I

PART II

Acknowledgment

My sincere gratitude to everyone who made this possible. Thank you so much for being a part of my ploughing journey.

<u>GLOSSARY</u>

<u>Brain:</u>

The organ inside the head that controls movement, thought, memory, and feeling

<u>Consciousness:</u>

The state of being able to use your senses and mental powers to understand what is happening
The state of being aware of something

<u>Conserve:</u>

To protect something and prevent it from being changed or destroyed

<u>Grow:</u>

To increase in size, number, strength, or quality

<u>Mind:</u>

(Noun) The part of a person that makes them able to be aware of things, to think and to feel
(Noun) Your ability to think and reason; your intelligence; the particular way that somebody thinks

<u>Plough:</u>

(Noun) A large piece of farming equipment with one or several curved blades (= metal cutting parts), pulled by a tractor or by animals. It is used for digging and turning over soil, especially before seeds are planted.

(Verb) To dig and turn over a field or other area of land with a plough

<u>Thought:</u>
(Noun) The small hard part produced by a plant, from which a new plant can grow

<u>Weed:</u>
A wild plant growing where it is not wanted, especially among crops or garden plants

Idioms

<u>Plough your own furrow:</u>
To do things that other people do not do, or be interested in things that other people are not interested in
To do something in isolation; to act without the help or influence of others.

<u>Plough on:</u>
To move, progress, or develop at a slow but constant and deliberate pace, especially that which is menial, time consuming, or tedious.

<u>Plough through (something):</u>
To create a path through some heavy substance with or as with a plough
To progress through something with great speed, enthusiasm, or determination

<u>Plough the sand:</u>
Labour uselessly

<u>Put your hand to the plough:</u>
Embark on a task.

<u>*Stop ploughing the sand, put your hands to the plough, plough your own furrow, plough on, and plough through this life.*</u>

Dr. Anuruti Rai

FIND YOUR WHY

FIND YOUR WHY

Working on yourself is a lifelong phenomenon. Before you begin reading this book, I want you to commit to the process and FIND YOUR WHY.

Refer to this page whenever you continue reading the next time, and every time.

Ponder over the following questions and answer them for yourself. Leave them empty if you don't know the answers just now. Come back later when you're ready.

1. Why is it that you wish to understand your thinking realm? Why do you want to change the way you think? Write down the reason here. Take time to answer this for yourself.

....

....

....

2. Who is the only person who can help you on this journey? Write down YOUR name here for future reference. A reminder here that our innermost selves always stand alone.

. . . .

Therefore, whenever you think you cannot control how you think or feel, refer to point number 2, and whenever you don't see a reason to change the way you react to life, refer to point number 1.

Remember that your potential is much more than anyone ever permitted you to believe.

PREFACE

<u>MY JOURNEY OF MIND OVER MATTER</u>

Can you recall the moment in your life when you first learned about your Mind? I can make it easier for you to answer this by hinting that there is no right or wrong answer. You've always known about it. No one introduced it to you. The habit of listening to worldly others and then speaking to yourself about the matters that mean the most to you wasn't taught to you. You and your Mind have never been separate entities. You've always known each other and worked together harmoniously.

However, the uncertainty and pace of the world today are fast changing the equation we have with our minds. With 'artificial intelligence' taking over our 'good-old prudence', and 'the noise galore' taking away the 'solitude with self' cherished earlier, a sorted version of our brilliant working minds is indeed a luxury! Very few of you will be able to honestly deny that the most ignored and often overlooked friend you have is you.

In this book, I have, in my utmost sincerity, tried to help you gain some sense of your mind and brain duo. I invite you to imagine the possibilities that could emerge if you understood the exact way your mind functions! What if you could discover how your Mind works like a watchmaker knows how the watch ticks or the IT expert can troubleshoot computer problems?

Before diving into the Mind Sea, let me introduce you to my journey of learning to understand the Mind. I am aware of this being an unusual introduction to a book about the Mind, but I'd still relate the truth to you.

It all began on my first day at the anatomy dissection hall. I'd never seen a lifeless human (called a cadaver in anatomy). Here I was, seeing one for the first time at seventeen and experiencing mixed emotions (primarily negative) never known or understood hitherto. This was the first time I realized that each life awaits an inevitable end. The reality stared me straight in the eye. Seeing this gentleman in eternal slumber created such turmoil in me that I began questioning why I'd never really cherished life up until now. Also, on the contrary, life had lost its meaning for me as I saw that it did cease to exist.

I called my dad after the demonstration and asked, "What is life about Papa if all of us have to die one day?" He sensed the confusion in my voice, took a long pause, and replied, "Life is worthwhile because it will end one day, and assuming that day is far, continue to give your best!"
I tried to seep in his wise words in a shaken state of mind, and it took me a few pensive weeks to overcome the perplexity.

The sole question that remained with me was, do I understand life? I looked for answers in all the places I had hoped to find them, and in the course of that search, I luckily found something I wasn't even looking for but made more sense to me.

Why should I try to understand life? I thought to myself. I needed to learn to make the most of it. I figured that if I just studied medicine to understand human ailments and treat them, it wouldn't be integral to a cause. I wanted to appreciate my body's functioning to be able to empathize and treat with others going through illnesses. Understanding myself first will be a testament that I can fully understand others too and help them. As providence had it, the first organ I was going to learn about was the human brain.

The upcoming dissection was of the head and neck region. The final aim of removing the brain from the human skull began with reflecting the layers of the scalp. The scalp is the covering over the bony skull, which needs to be carefully removed to reach the skull cap. It took a team of ten of us about two hours to reveal the bony skull while keenly observing and uncovering each layer. It was an exhilarating experience to witness the ultimate human packaging and I was in my mind celebrating how intricately nature built us. I was instantly reminded of how nature knows best. I was once told in my childhood that only a banana peel could keep the banana fresh for days and preserve its goodness, unlike any man-made packaging.

The next dissection was about removing the skull cap and separating the brain from its bodily attachments. This exercise made my curiosity grow further, as I learned that this is the only bone in the body to encase an entire vital organ.

It took us a couple of sessions to mark and learn the path of each cranial nerve being sectioned in the process.

Eventually, the day I had this magnificent brain in front of me, I felt like a five-year-old looking at a completed superfluous jigsaw puzzle. Little did I know then that the brain needed to be well protected because of the energy (Mind) it is capable of generating.

Finally contented that my questions about the anatomy of the human brain were answered, I felt utterly grateful to this man, who once had a life, relationships, and a purpose of his own. He helped me learn anatomy and made me realize that neither two brains are identical, nor are they entirely different. I wondered how complicated yet simple we are, stitched with flawless threads invisible in entirety, beautiful, diverse, and uniquely reimagined by the supreme nature that created us.

What struck me suddenly was that this gentleman on the steel bed had a brain, but where was his mind? The brain and the mind no longer meant the same to me.

I wanted to decipher the Mind now! The bigger mystery that fascinated me was how humans use this organ to make each life so unique. I set out on a mission to crack the complex code of mental functioning and the causes behind the same. The most straightforward path to understanding the mind machinery was to understand the ability of different minds to respond to standardized stimuli.

However, standardization of neither the mind nor the stimuli was possible. No two brains are created the same and no two brains receive the same environment to grow, learn and experience, even in siblings as well as twins.

While researching reactions to similar stimuli among individuals, such as fear, pressure, rejection, failure, and success, the feedback was mind-boggling. The findings and conclusions made it clear that no two brains respond in a similar fashion to external influences in life. Further studies revealed numerous factors responsible for why humans react differently to replicated stimuli.

The key determinant, however, responsible for our uniqueness turned out to be the playground we visit every day to play our favourite game of thinking with and talking to ourselves.

I have to admit that though I haven't found all the answers I was looking for, yet, I have indeed found where to look for the answers.

The sole endeavour of this book is to let you understand your Mind's thinking and decision-making machinery. This book is deliberately divided into two parts. Part I is all about knowing yourself and getting familiar with tools your already own to finally reach Part II and set out to plough to your full potential. In a distraction-laden world, stop wasting your brain's energy reacting mindlessly to external influences beyond your control. Look within and look beyond your circumstances at present, then will you learn your life's purpose. History has proved time and again that anything unbelievable yet imaginable is achievable.

All the people I have been able to help were proactively willing to help themselves. By reaching their inner beings and addressing their-inner selves (without external judgment altering and governing their choices), they discovered the mechanism of working of their Minds and fought for themselves against their older selves.

Our minds have fallen into the trap of mediocrity with every sunset simply because we have forgotten what it is capable of. Let us preserve our inner genius before they fall into the trap of believing themselves to be ordinary.

PART I

PART I

1. Do you understand yourself? 

 2. Simplifying the mind

3. Thinking with clarity 

1.
DO YOU UNDERSTAND YOURSELF?

THE IRONY OF HUMAN LIFE!

Consider the following statement,

y is a function of x
$y=y(x)$

The above equation denotes a condition where the value of "y" varies according to whatever value "x" takes on. For example, the price of a box of ten chocolates(y) will vary with the cost of each chocolate in the box(x). If each chocolate costs two rupees, the cost of the box will be half of what it will be as compared to when each chocolate costs 4 rupees.

You do not need to understand the derivation or complexity of this equation. You just need to learn one simple and clear message it conveys to you as a human.

You are not a box of chocolates and do not need to weigh your self-worth with external scales.

Have you ever wondered if your self-worth is a function of what others say, feel, hate, or love about you? If yes, Then it is high time you realize that the above equation does not hold true for you.

Consider this: if someone likes you, you believe that you must be a likable person but the very next moment, if someone ridicules you, you are left with no confidence to face the world. Sounds familiar?

Imagine the magnitude of value you tend to associate with the versions of you that others have defined for you. You keep attaching these identities that don't even belong to you, to your self-image.

I'll go to the extent of saying that they are merely cages of self-consciousness gifted to us without our consent. And, to our misery, we tend to treasure them.

Do you know the root cause of our reckless tendency to believe in external judgements rather than internal beliefs? ***Lack of basic knowledge of self!***

Most of us do not know ourselves in the first place. Human social psychology is so enigmatic that a character certificate is valued more than self-belief. We know ourselves as a function of what others say, like, or hate about us. If we keep changing ourselves to keep the equation valid, then we're treading on the deadly path of self-betrayal and emotional suicide.

I am addressing this phenomenon at the very beginning because this is the first step towards knowing yourself, by deleting all the stored versions of you (in your mind) that others have specified for you.

They define you before you can define yourself

The above illustration shows how, when we are born, we are given a name, an identity, and a burden of expectations even before we begin to know ourselves. You are not always what they say about you.

UNDERSTANDING THE SELF

Learning something new in life does not come without discovering a thing or two about yourself in the process. Therefore, to understand our thinking machinery, let us dive into the depths of evolution and revive our definition of ourselves. I will not puzzle you with complicated medical terminology (there are excellent books on that already).

The first step in learning about your mind is learning about your being, your world, and the interactions between the two.

OUR BEING (WHO ARE WE?)

A Human being, i.e. your being and my being, are broadly a conjugation of two things

1. The five senses
   The senses (and associated organs) pick up the necessary information from the outside world,

2. Intelligence Centre
   The intelligence centre (with related organs) interprets this information as the survival probability report!

That's all we are! Nothing more and nothing short of a miracle! Every organ other than the above merely aids in survival but without the above two, survival is questionable.

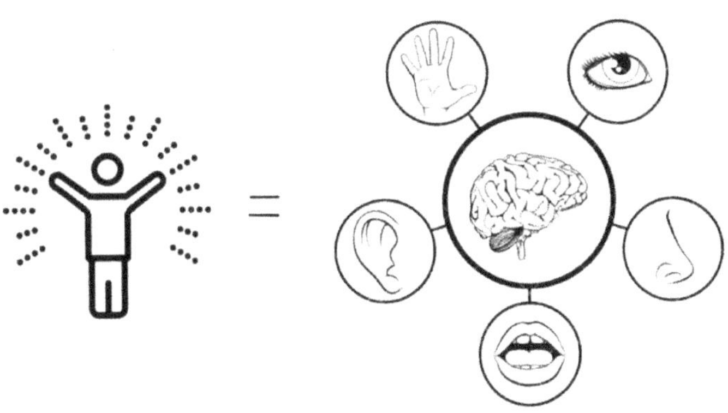

Our being $=$ Intelligence + special senses

If you think this is too scientific/boring, remember we are precisely that.

This simple definition of yourself, when repeated to yourself time and again, will make life much simpler for you. We stand alone in this world to survive and thrive and are equipped with the essential prerequisites for both.

Nature has bestowed us not only with survival instincts but also the best of our abilities. This applies not only to humans but to other species as well. It is interesting to note how Elephants can sense rainstorms up to 150 miles away because that is a survival skill set for them! A more rare ability is noted in Axolotl, an amphibian, which can regenerate its lost limbs, tail, jaws, spinal cord, and even parts of the brain and skin.

What, in your opinion, is so remarkable and enviable in humans that make us the most powerful species on this planet?
Our ability to reason.

The power to reason makes it possible for you to plan and create your future. Your brilliant mind is super adaptive, making you open to progressive change and planning ahead of time.

HOW DOES REASON WORK?

The five senses are designed to fetch cues from the outside world. These cues initiate some thought/emotion/idea or action within us and are called stimuli (singular: stimulus). Every favourable stimulus does not incite a prompt positive response in the first course of interaction with a being. This, however, can be changed with consistent practice and knowledge. For instance, your taste buds may not approve of bitter gourd and greens, but once you know how beneficial it is for your body, you welcome them into your diet. Similarly, challenges usually lead to tension or worry, and our brain tries to avoid them until we recognize how they make us grow hence training our minds to embrace them.

<u>OUR WORLD</u>

The world for your being is all the meaningful cues that surround you. I say meaningful because everything around you does not incite a response from you. This closed system of you and your world makes your life and experiences possible.

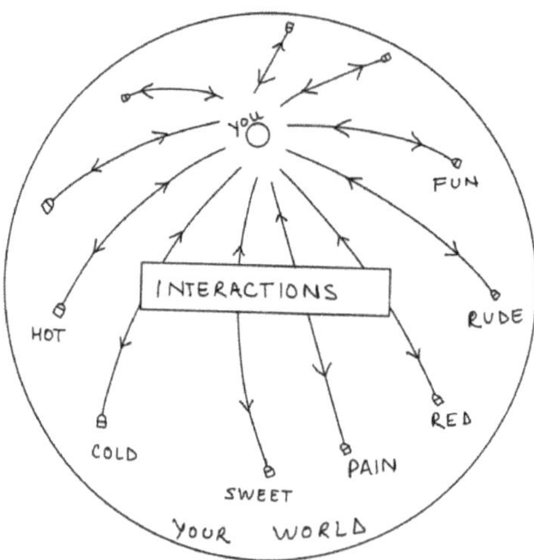

The interactions between your being and your world are termed life

Our world = Our being + (collection of stimuli)

If you look closely at the above equation, you will understand that the entire world for us is merely an assortment of stimuli! If you look back at the life you've lived, you have only experienced and responded to stimuli all this while.

In today's world, with so much on your plate to digest, you must aim to be a priority to yourself. It is as vital to your well-being as breaking the false image of you governed by worldly expectations. One needs to understand that success's definition is not universal. Had it been so, everyone would have wanted the exact same things from life and would have had zero ambition once those things were achieved, and hence mankind's growth and evolution would have come to a standstill.

Life in broader terms is lived inside your head. The brain is where all the experiences happen, and the mind is where the responses generate. That's precisely how your brain is created and your mind functions. Humans directly or indirectly are just aiming for survival, with the senses that help us in choosing favourable stimuli all our life! However, you will agree, that the process is not really so simple. Moving forwards is more than just stepping ahead, it also involves pushing yourself when the road gets rocky and your body is heavy with thoughts of despair weighing you down. We need to deal with our emotions and positively heal ourselves, make ourselves ready for the future and simultaneously deal with the past that affects us. And that is, a lot more than barely surviving, to say the least.

Let us undertake this inward journey to solve the mind maze and reveal where your superpowers remain neglected. Nature gave you one left and one right hand so that you can always shake hands with yourself first!

May you love your being more, learn your mind better, befriend yourself and win at your game. If you merely realize and respect your intellect today, future civilizations will take care of themselves.

<u>TAKEAWAY NOTES</u>

- We know ourselves as a function of what others think about us. We need to break this false image of ourselves, in order to understand who we truly are.

- A being is made up of the five senses and an intelligence centre.

- The senses pick up the necessary information from the outside world, and the intelligence centre interprets this information as the survival probability report.

- The ability to reason is the most remarkable power bestowed upon human beings.

- The entire world for a being is nothing but an assortment of stimuli.

- If your mind is working well, it will resolve the problems and act towards the solutions. If not, then your survival becomes questionable.

2.
SIMPLIFYING THE CONCEPT OF MIND

HOW THE MIND ELUDES US

Nikita studied hard and performed well in her exams but feared not making it to the top. She often cried her heart out in dismay while the results were awaited. Finally, when the results were declared, she did excel and topped her university!! When interviewed about her success, she didn't appear happy and kept stressing that acing the university didn't mean much to her as she didn't score a 100 in her favourite subject.

Was this justified? Maybe! Can we learn something from this example? Definitely! It is interesting to note how our mind eludes us! This is exactly how we delay our happiness as we program our minds for life. We might not think of ourselves as being worthy of recognition, but, when we do get it, we always want more.

The mind of a human is characterized to be the most unsettled and unpredictable instrument. The restless nature of the mind makes a human continuously seek fulfilment of one wish and the moment that wish is fulfilled, the mind spontaneously starts yearning for the next one. Whether you agree or not, this is the condition of most of our minds. But, is it justified to treat two minds alike or even define them under similar criteria?

I wasn't surprised when my research on the ability of different minds to deal with similar situations resulted in non-coherent results each time. What puzzled me was what makes us use our brains so differently. Let us understand with an easy example. For instance, If we equate the brain to a camera, how do two photographers shoot absolutely unique pictures? This is because the images captured by exactly the same cameras depend entirely on the perspective, choices, and complex colour play by the photographer even when the object to be shot is also the same. The reason behind this is what interests them! The same applies to our mind's perspective of life. Almost everyone has similar brain models but clicks very different pictures because the mind is what we make of the brain that we are provided with at birth.

You may have been juvenile and could not control your circumstances from the start. You may have been naïve while getting to know the world and wondering at its expanse, but what you chose to store as memories was mostly up to you. The decision to choose what you want to remember for tomorrow is absolutely intentional. The photographs that you wish to keep are saved and often cherished and the ones that hold little importance are deleted, pretty much like a camera.

Here, I also want to emphasize the fact that taking good pictures could be an inborn talent or deliberately achieved after honing your skills. The same is possible for the brain too. Either you were born with a brain programmed for a happy life or you constantly choose to work on yourself to keep the best of your memories to yourself, just like a learning photographer.

BRAIN AS OPPOSED TO MIND

The dilemma I faced after my life's first-ever dissection was one that stayed with me for quite a long time. The terms brain and mind are often used interchangeably in most literature except in medicine. We have learnt that the brain is a physical entity and the mind is its abstract power. The brain is composed of neurons and other supporting cells while the mind is defined by non-figurative and often less defined realms. A brain can be seen physically or visualized in the form of scans, however, there is no way in which a human can envision someone else's mind.

The enigmatic nature of the mind can be distinguished from the brain using very simple metaphors. If we think of the brain as a magnet then the mind will be its magnetism.

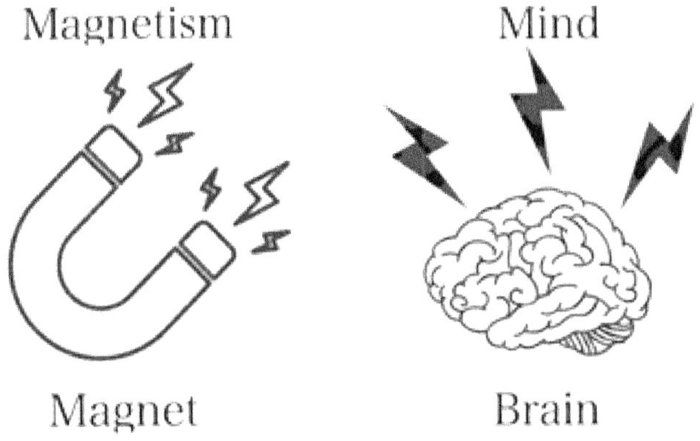

A magnet attracts iron by virtue of its magnetic field. The brain performs its tasks by virtue of the thinking mind. A magnet is defined by its characteristic property of magnetism in the same way as the brain is defined by the uniqueness of its mind. A magnet that has lost its magnetism is nothing more than a piece of metal quite like the brain that has lost its ability to think with the mind.

The brain is a platform where the thinking takes place, and the thinking takes place as a result of the Mind. The Mind makes thinking possible!
Just like a needle cannot hold a torn cloth together but it can help the thread sew it. Similarly, the mind helps the brain do what is asked of it.

Technically, your brain is the hardware, and your mind is the software. The hardware holds little importance without the software. Your mind is the realm of your brain, which isn't matter, but matters the most!

We have tiny worlds of our own encased in our very strong skulls and beyond it, just like the earth is incomplete without the atmosphere, the brain is incomplete without the Mind. How and where we were born is not under our control, but what we grasp and where we stand in the world definitely is.

Though the cranial capacities in humans are comparable, it's our mind which differentiates how we think and feel and therefore creates our distinctive perspectives and lives.

One thing common to humans which played a significant role in diversifying evolution is our opposable thumbs, but our complex mind has made it possible for all mankind to derive a variety of unique uses of the opposable thumb in order to make our creativity and imagination come to life. Hence, there's no denying that the mind ideal for you was gifted to you; what you do with it is your gift to this world!!

<u>BRAIN MIND INTERACTION!</u>

The brain and mind may be separate entities in form and definition but they work together seamlessly to give our thinking the marvellous speed greater than a rocket and even light. While light travels at the rate of 186000 miles per second, our thoughts travel in virtually no time.
Whatever the body experiences and gathers is transmitted to the brain in the form of chemical and electrical signals. Given the speed of thought, it takes no time for the brain to decide the next move in the form of a response to an experience.

However, this entire exchange of the stimulus and response is converted in the mind in the form of meaningful thoughts and stored in the brain for future reference.

The following illustration depicts how when stimuli are relayed to the brain, the Mind creates meaningful stories of all that is fed to it.

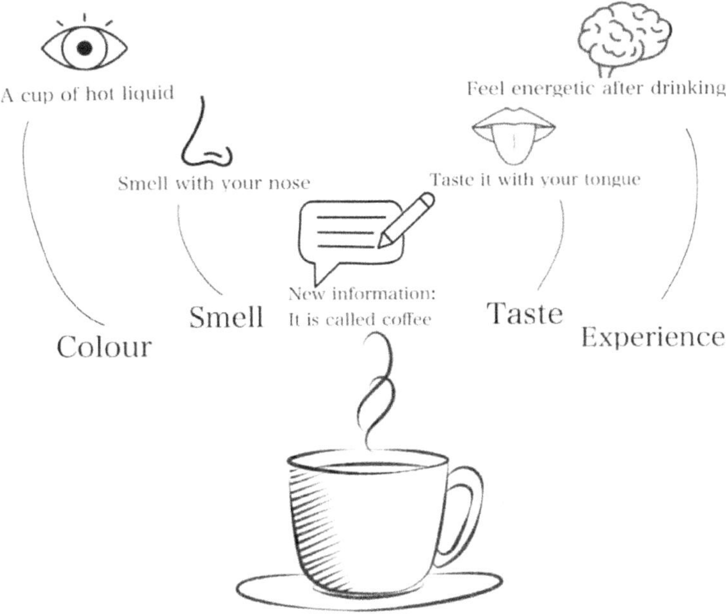

In the above illustration, the brain experiences drinking coffee for the first time with a bunch of new information to store in the mind for future reference.

<u>HOW ARE TWO MINDS DIFFERENT?</u>

Our life experiences form our neural pathways; hence no two minds are the same. This is to say that whenever we need to make a choice, our conscious choice will depend on our previous life experiences and the thinking skills we have developed from them.

All that you choose is a result of all that you are willing to give up on or consciously abandon.
This is an important reason why a lot of importance is attached to first experiences.

Following the example of the previous illustration,
Some people might not like the taste of coffee or don't like the after feeling of having a coffee so they make amendments in their schedule to avoid depending on it for an energy boost. Every stimulus incites unique responses from different minds and hence everyone has a different take on the exact same situation.

This is one reason why every person reading this book will experience it differently!

<u>THE LIMITLESS MIND</u>

Look around and you'll be convinced that all the ground-breaking inventions and discoveries made in history, and all of the progress made in the field of various arts have been done by people who never considered their minds to be bound by limits.

They chose to push forth their limits against present circumstances because they never stopped believing that what is deemed impossible today, will be a normal tomorrow.

What caused humans to stop walking and think hard to imagine and create a wheel? What made humankind not only fly but also explore space? – the stubbornness to anticipate and work for a future they regarded to be true.

This is evidence that it is only you, who is actively involved in setting limits for your mind because nature never created any!

<u>WHAT DETERMINES YOUR MIND'S LIMIT??</u>

There was a riddle I remember being asked as a kid. What can reach anywhere before you do? I didn't understand why the answer to the riddle was the "mind" until much later.

Researchers say an average brain can store up to 2.5 million GB of digital memory in it. In simpler words, it means that our brain can store up to 3 million hours of digital video data; which is to say that a healthy brain never runs out of memory.

If your brain and mind are limitless, why aren't you superhuman? Why is the limit of the human brain exactly how much it accepts it to be?

There are two reasons for that:
1. We question our abilities. We believe that all we have is what we were born with and nothing can be changed.
2. Nature has limited the three constants of our life to balance our limitless minds.
Namely,

1. Time(limited but same for everyone)
2. Energy(limited but can be comparable for two beings)
3. Consciousness (the deciding factor for what your Mind can do for you)

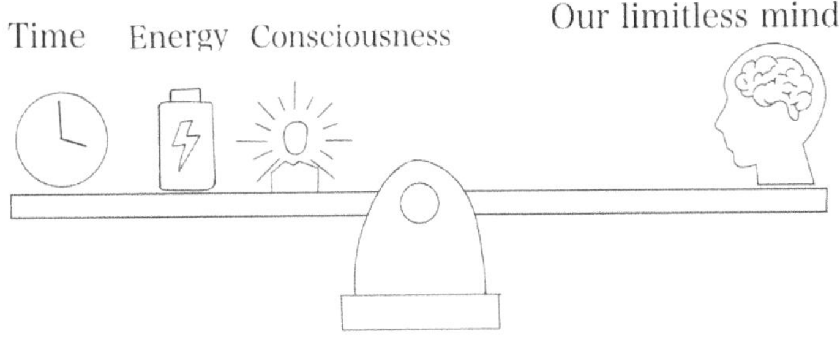

Of the three constants listed above about what determines our Mind's limits, the limits posed by time and energy to our true potential are self-explanatory. We cannot work on a project beyond a deadline and we cannot work within the deadline if we are out of energy to function. I want to elaborate on the importance of consciousness because that's the reason for two minds to be different even when they have the exact same brains. Will two identical twins lead identical lives? No, because of the ultimate force of <u>consciousness.</u>

I remember a story of two brothers from school. One of the brothers grew up to be an alcoholic and the other a successful billionaire. The alcoholic son blamed their father for his addiction while the billionaire thanked his dad for showing him exactly what not to do with his life. One witnessed the habit and ingrained it and the other saw the outcome and abstained! This is one great example of how our consciousness can create or devastate us.

<u>UNDERSTANDING YOUR CONSCIOUSNESS</u>

Consciousness, per se, is a complex state of being to gain an understanding of. Trying to make it simpler to grasp was only possible with the help of a metaphor to make the concept come to life and etch your visual brain area to keep a note of it.

THE MIND-SEA MODEL

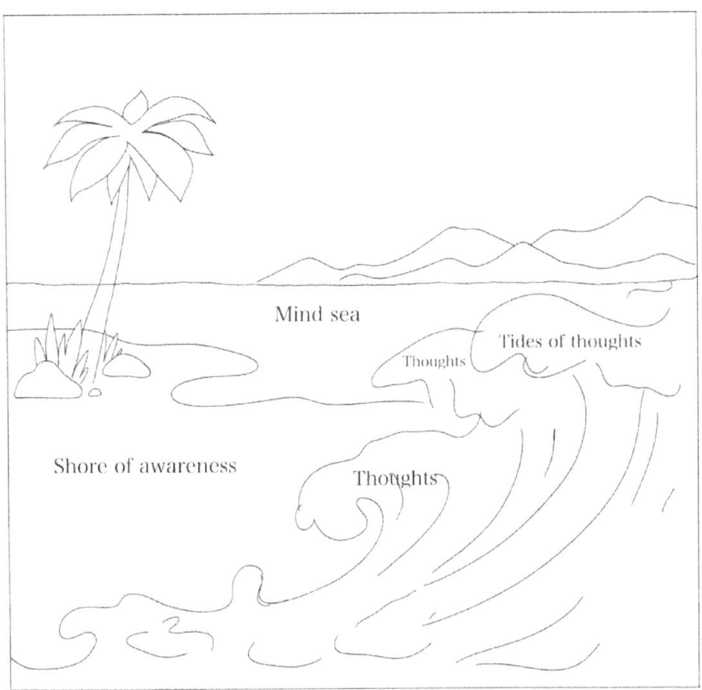

In the illustration above,
Mind=sea
Thoughts=tides
Sand/shore= awareness

Imagine your mind as a sea, vast and boundless with tides of thoughts gushing over the shores of your awareness. All the tides differ in strength and pattern just like your thoughts. Sometimes, the minor tides bring about fleeting thoughts to nudge you to perform daily routine activities. However, only the strong tides (deep, immersive thoughts) have the ability to cause some real change in the seashore of your awareness and bring about realizations that get etched in the sands. They bring about real transformation.

In another flow of thoughts, the minor tides reach up to collide with the shores of your awareness more often than necessary to repeatedly reinforce unimportant thoughts(i.e. memory clutter, living in the past, etc), while strong tides with enough force of bringing a better change in you die down even before touching the sands.

Whichever of the above two states you believe your mind to be in, for a larger part of the day, just remember that with the innumerable tides raging every minute, only the ones that repeatedly and frequently touch your shores will create a stir of change in you. They define your personality and character.

Now imagine a lighthouse that guides you to focus on the major tides of the sea and serves as a navigational aid! This lighthouse represents our consciousness. Our brains may be similar, but our minds are not because of the guiding lighthouse of consciousness.

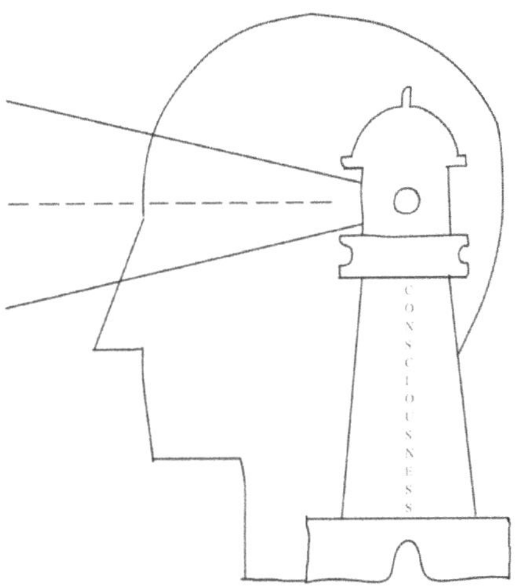

Quite literally, consciousness is your ability to use your Mind in real-time!

If you compare a surgeon performing heart surgery and the same surgeon fixing a leaking tap at his house, the exact same mind is engrossed in two different tasks of varying soft skills and attention.
Where our consciousness lies makes all the difference!!

The brain as we know is matter, whereas the Mind is energy. Nature protects your brain with a skull, and you must protect your Mind energy by conserving your consciousness. The need of the hour is to create an energy barrier for our minds against the overflowing information current which not only disrupts our consciousness but also, makes us addicted to the anticipation of what's new the next minute.

<u>CONSCIOUSNESS AS VALUABLE CURRENCY</u>

Once we have learnt about consciousness and how it guides us to make use / utilize our brainpower, I'd like you to understand how we spend our consciousness in a day.

Do you often think the day is too short for completing all of your tasks? Do you tend to waste half of your day on unimportant things and suddenly rocket to the end of your deadline at night? Doesn't it get impossible to complete a task when your mind is wandering elsewhere??
It is a prevalent practice to learn time management and plan your hours precisely to enjoy a productive day. Whereas the truth is that the only hack to a productive day is not just time management, but consciousness management.

<u>*We have a limited number of neurons; it's up to us what we make them do all day.*</u>

The following are some consciousness pie chart distributions to understand how we live through a day managing our consciousness.

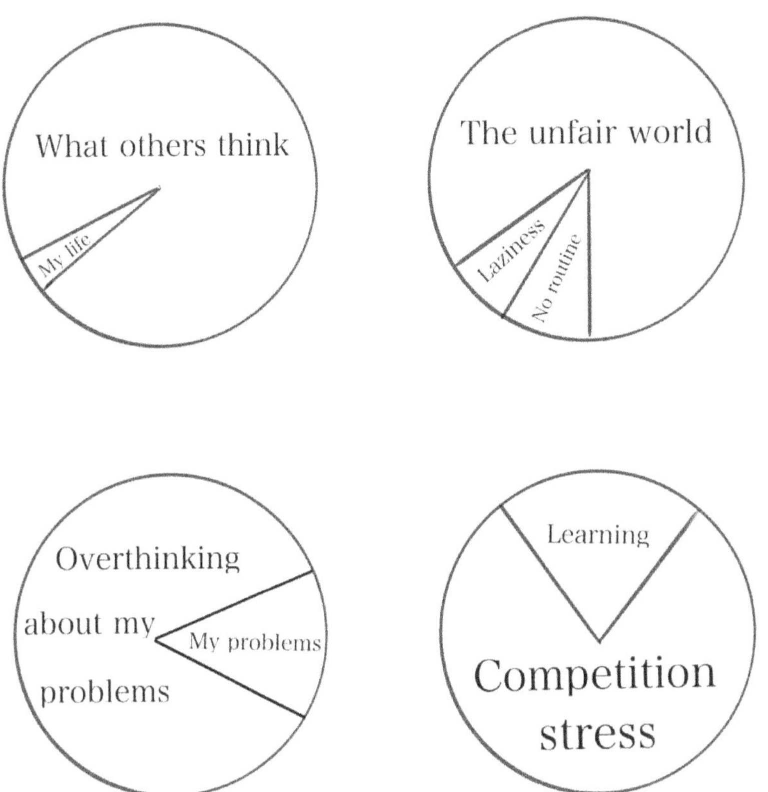

These pie charts depict how we devote our daily consciousness currency to vital, necessary, unnecessary, and rubbish stimuli. If you do not value your consciousness as valuable currency, then your lack of proactive efforts in being thoughtful about spending it results in making impulsive choices throughout the day. However, the worst possible scenario would be to wake up with yesterday's problem still in your Mind. That way, you will wake up with only 50 to 60 percent of available consciousness currency the next day!

A pattern of consciousness distribution thus observed is that if the everyday little problems occupy a large part of your conscious mind, you may not even realize the bigger problem you're getting yourself into, which is the loss of living while being alive!

Being considerate about how you spend your consciousness daily, is a learned art. It takes immense practice to be able to comb through countless life experiences and choose to respond to or ignore them diligently.

<u>Draw a pie chart of what takes up our consciousness every day. You will be surprised at how inconsistent the chart is each day.</u>

In order to be smarter about making these choices, my sincere advice to you would be to watch what you react to. There are situations in everyone's lives when you either react impulsively and end up regretting your ways or brood over some instances for too long. If you identify and understand the situations where you tend to react impulsively, you'll identify your consciousness thieves and learn to deal with them. As you work on yourself, you will realize how your consciousness pie chart shifts into depicting a more fulfilling day.

FIXATING YOUR CONSCIOUSNESS

Life is all about discovering this world and yourself. It took me years and years of looking for myself on this quest of learning about who I am. Looking back, I know one thing for sure, whatever challenged me changed me forever. Whenever unable to recollect something, I had this habit of shutting my ears and eyes to look for the answer to a question or a long-lost word (such as Chlamydomonas). Little did I know that this act essentially turned my consciousness inwards.

To listen to your inner self, you need to break free from self-posed limitations which sometimes come from your own senses. Your senses are designed to keep you updated about your surroundings and elicit a reaction/response from you. They need to be switched off or diminished at times to reach inside and dig out the wisdom stored in your memory for future reference(and even mugged up answers in an exam) I practiced it to calm my mind and sometimes seek out answers to questions I had studied years ago as a student. I even occasionally used it during my exams in school and they never failed me. This is one technique that came in handy to recollect anything that I'd heard or read, ever in my life.

What I was essentially doing was focussing /putting all of my mental energy into solving that particular problem. I e fixating my consciousness.

Little did I know then, that, what I was essentially doing was a form of meditation. I was looking for a particular answer while consciously shutting out all the noises. If you can train your Mind forcibly to think of nothing, it works with better focus rather than brooding over all the distractions that show up in the outside world!

<u>MEDITATION</u>

There is immense power in meditation, and I do not intend to recite about what your spiritual upliftment is capable of (though that's a virtue too). I want to bring your attention to the measurable benefits that meditation has to offer. There is no dearth of scientific research on stress reduction, anxiety control, improved memory, and better sleep quality as a result of meditation, among many others.

<u>The old belief that there is no alt + control + del for the brain is no longer valid. It has been decoded through meditation.</u>

Remember this, "Life will take you to places you've never been, the Mind will take you to thoughts you've never known, but you need to come back to yourself every day. " That's what meditation is.

If you're new to meditation, as all of us are, at some point in our life, we must simply try to be open-minded (pun intended) about it and watch it work wonders for us. When we start something new, it feels overwhelming but when we start to notice the positive changes it brings in us, we get habituated to the growth. Meditation is like exercise, no one else can do it for you. That's one good reason why the destination of inner peace is the same, the path through the meditation may be different for individuals. Some like guided meditations, calming music works for some and some prefer to be in nature's lap while listening to nature sounds.

I would like to share with you my favourite meditation. The reason why it is my favourite is that I practiced them without even being aware of what meditation was. This is the meditation that I find simple enough for beginners to follow through with and effective enough for the pros. It does not require any gadgets or apps; just a combination of concentration and introspection.

PHOSPHENE MEDITATION

This was my most enjoyable pass time as a student. I never liked sleeping in the afternoons after lunch. When everyone was asleep, I would lie against the window and close my eyes to see the most wonderful patterns of merging colours. It was such a joyous experience that my mind followed the colours and forgot about worldly events like fights with friends, science tests, etc. It was so much fun to know that I could escape my homework worries and witness the dance of colours and light with closed eyes. When everyone woke up, I felt as fresh as after a good afternoon nap.

These blobs of colourful light seen when we close our eyes are called phosphenes. The colours get intensified by rubbing the eyes.

So next time you need some time to yourself, close your eyes and admire the phosphenes. It is the easiest way to think about nothing as thinking about nothing is the most difficult thing to do.

NEUROPLASTICITY

Ever wondered about the ability of the brain to change itself and how much can it change? Scientists call this phenomenon Neuroplasticity, i.e., the ability of the adult brain to change itself. Studies have proved that this is possible not only in a healthy brain but also in a damaged one. The instances where brain tissue was wounded due to trauma or had to be removed surgically have also shown magnificent improvements which are remarkable examples of how the brain can change itself. The ability of an adult brain to change opens up a whole world of possibilities. The term neuroplasticity denotes that the brain can be changed; but what exactly changes the brain?

Our brain is mainly shaped by two things: external stimulus (from the outer world) and our response (from the inner world)

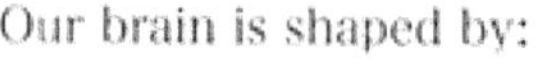

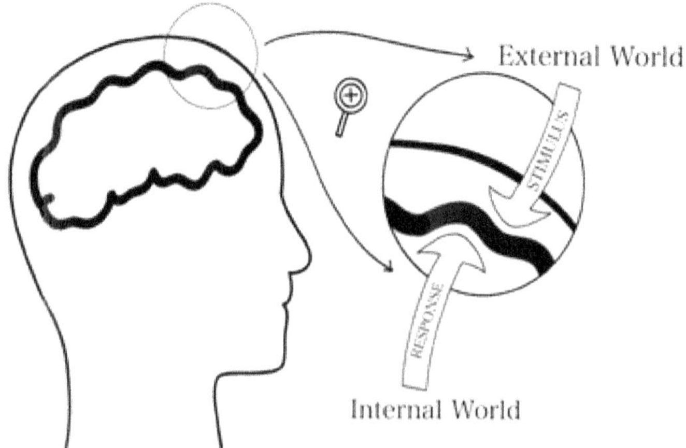

Our responses to the outer world and the subsequent thoughts generated shape our brains. As a result of our life experiences, the very structure of our brain changes depending on how we lived and what we faced. The brain is physically imprinted with the thoughts we have had, the decisions we have made, the skills we have learned and the actions we have taken.

The brain can change as a result of the thoughts that we have thought. Brain creates thoughts! But now, we must also know that changing the thinking and hence creating new thoughts can also change the brain.

Before the 1960s, researchers believed that the changes in the brain could only take place during the early growth years of infancy and childhood. There was a firm belief that by the phase of early adulthood, the brain's physical structure and neuronal circuit connections are mostly permanent, or in other words, the brain becomes hardwired and cannot be further changed.

Modern research has demonstrated that the brain is more malleable than previously believed. It continues to create new neural connections and pathways and change the existing ones as a result of new experiences, exposure to new information, and building new memories.

Neuroplasticity is no buzzword anymore. It is a term that refers to the brain's ability to change and adapt as a result of experience. The term neuroplasticity is derived from two words, neuro which refers to the brain cells or neurons, and plasticity, which refers to the ability to change its form or being mouldable.

Hence, the term is used to denote the brain's ability to be changed, influenced, and controlled as a result of the lives that we have led.

Research has also shown that the mental abilities of humans continue to be enhanced as a result of their efforts, to the extent that even damaged brains can exhibit remarkable transformation.

Neuroplasticity is of the following two types:

i.   Functional Plasticity (altering functional aspects): the changes in the brain's functional aspects, i.e. recruitment of a different undamaged region of the brain to take control of a certain activity after suffering damage to the original centre.

ii. Structural Plasticity (altering physical aspects such as shape and form): the brain's ability to change its physical structure as a result of learning new information and storing new memories.

The more and more we practice the piano, for example, the more and more the brain networks responsible for musical dexterity and fine motor sensations areas of the fingers will strengthen.

This plasticity of the brain is beneficial in:

i. the ability to learn and master new skills with practice.

ii. the ability to upgrade your present intellectual and creative skills

iii. the power to recover from brain injuries and strokes.

iv. strengthening the brain areas after loss or decline in function

v. improvements that can enhance brains strength and productivity

Since the mind is mightier than the brain, a change in the mind can change the brain. Therefore, if we devote more time to shifting our consciousness day after day, the brain will change itself pertaining to what is asked of it.

The mere knowledge of Neuroplasticity and its benefits makes it seem so simple and doable to consciously change our brains. Then why aren't all of us practicing it and changing our inner and outer world already?? Let's find out what stops us in the next chapter.

<u>TAKEAWAY NOTE!</u>

- The brain is a platform where the thinking takes place, and the thinking takes place as a result of the Mind.

- We have tiny worlds of our own encased in our very strong skulls and beyond it, just like the earth is incomplete without the atmosphere, the brain is incomplete without the mind!

- Our life experiences form our neural pathways; hence no two minds are the same.

- Only you can transform your brain if you make up your mind.

- While minds and brains are created as limitless, nature has limited our time, energy, and consciousness to balance the equation!

- When your consciousness reaches the depth of your mind's ocean, that's when you truly begin to understand your being.

- Life will take you to places you've never been, and the mind will take you to thoughts you've never known, but you need to come back to yourself every day. That's what mediation is.

- Whatever the brain experiences and gathers, it stores in the mind, when the mind is mightier than the brain, a change in mind can change the brain.

- The latest research shows time and again that we can change our brains by altering our thoughts. Let us embrace this fact and work on ourselves!

- If we devote more time to improving ourselves day after day, the brain will change itself pertaining to what is asked of it.

3.
THINKING WITH CLARITY

What is your idea of evolution? Do you think humans are evolving lately? A necessity for evolution is the skill to change ourselves with the changing times. If we've managed to study the human brain to the extent that we have evidence that it can be changed, why has nothing significant changed about our learning, thinking, or behavioural patterns?

The human mind was programmed to seek safety and comfort even before the Stone Age. All of the developments carried out by mankind in the name of civilization were based on the principle of safety and sustainability of the human race. Humans created weapons to counter predators, built huts to be sheltered from harsh weather, and began cultivation to avoid hunting for food; all for comfort! Our intellect guides us to steer away from danger at all costs, even today when there are much fewer life-threatening dangers compared to the prehistoric era.

Why does a voice in your head pleads and reasons with you to skip your workout as you're tired and drowsy? Who tells you it is acceptable to have that dessert because you have earned it through your hard work? Who is convincing you that another binge-watch is necessary for the name of self-love? - Your pre-programmed mind, which hates change! At all costs, your health, your money, your time!

The hardest battle to win is against your pre-programmed mind!

You regularly fall into the mind's trap of inflexibility, and genuinely believe that your mind is trying to protect you from a muscle sprain, a missed delicacy, or a cool discussion with friends, as per the examples above. But, what is happening is, that you are not thinking clearly as your mind is biased. And with so much going on in our lives, we tend to choose the easy way out unless we've practiced and practiced to think with clarity!

The ultimate knowledge in this universe is the knowledge of self. We've been endowed with the senses to understand our surroundings. However, these special senses get so drowned in experiencing the world that we forget to understand and experience what a marvellous creation we are!

In short, Life gets the best of us!

ORGANIZING A BOOKSHELF

If you were to organize a bookshelf, how would you do it? Won't you keep your favourite books, books you refer to a lot, world atlases, dictionaries, a new book that you've been meaning to read, at the eye level? This way they will be easier to find and remind you often of their existence. Maybe keep the other subjects you study or books of high value you like to refer to once in a while on the next shelf. The most distant and difficult-to-reach shelf could hold the books you are not interested to read or the ones you wish to donate.

My question here is, why wouldn't you do the same with your thoughts!!

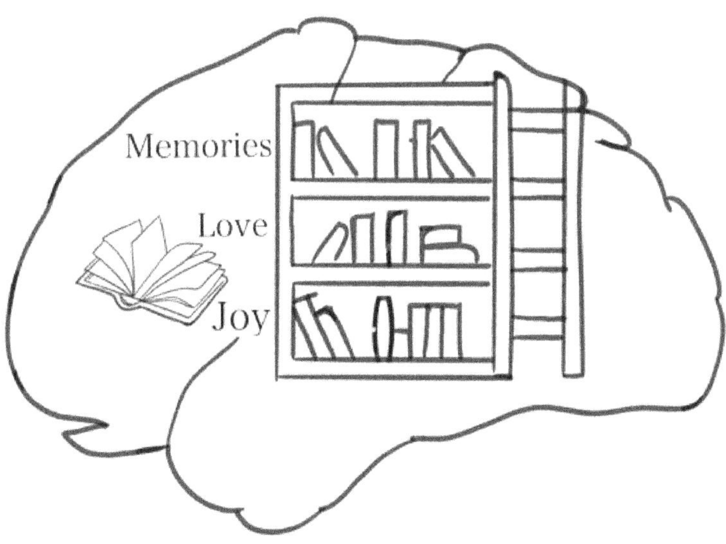

For example, everyone wants to be happy, but how many of you keep the happy thoughts and reminders closest to your consciousness? How many of us are consciously ready to choose joy every day no matter what?

Why won't we start managing what we engulf every day into our thinking realm and give away and forget about what doesn't serve us anymore?

The need of the hour, is, technically, to delete some trash files and silence some sounds in our minds, so we can finally focus on what means the most to us. If we could achieve it even for a single hour, our efficiency would become manifold.

THOUGHTS

All that you hold in your brain as memories today once originated as a string of thoughts. Your thoughts serve as the vehicles to generate the memory centres. Often wondered how a particular song reminds you of someone, or the smell of a favourite dish takes you back to your childhood? It is only due to the power of thoughts that are linked together in the most magnificent ways so you never fail to relive an entire incident in your head. This is exactly why avid fiction readers enjoy books that give them the details to live, experience, and cherish.

For example, lunch at a café is not as exciting and worth remembering as lunch on a sunny afternoon in a small riverside café of fresh crisp vegetable salad with cream cheese dressing. I am sure the latter chalks out a vivid picture in your imagination. That's exactly how memory works.

<u>INFORMATION</u>

Information as the term suggests comes to us from phones, television, the internet, etc. We have so much information to acquire that we have no time, attention span, or cognitive ability to process it.

When the inflow of information is regulated and filtered, its consequences to our thinking processes can be managed responsibly as opposed to when random information is bombarded to us from every possible source and direction, every working hour. This results in a false perception that we require all of the information that exists.

INFORMATION OVERLOAD

The way information was passed from one generation to the next was greatly through verbal means. Books and scriptures were also handwritten and preserved well to make sure that the ancient wisdom was secure and available to future students. To learn about a particular subject, the student had to follow one book and assimilate its contents.

It was that simple, and that difficult. I think of it as simple because there was no need to hunt for data or information elsewhere as the books were complete compendiums in themselves. However, the difficult part about imbibing information ages ago was getting hold of that one book with merely a few copies existing all over the world.

How contrasting is this to today's world??
The most knowledgeable books may be hiding somewhere deep in the shelves, while the uncertain and mostly untrue rumours can reach you the fastest via one click of a button.

The problems arising from information overload faced by us in today's time are more serious than you think. The amount of information is so vast these days that we cannot process and utilize it effectively. You get at least millions of articles, videos, images, and infographics showing you how to solve your problem, however, no amount of intelligent keywords can save you from getting drowned in the information flood online. You certainly do not have the time and energy to go through all of the data presented to you and oftentimes, it is only after intense research, can you judge whether the information is truly authentic.

THINKING CYCLES

Where do these thoughts originate? The stimuli from the world inspire our brain to create a meaningful version of what surrounds us and store it in the brain as a memory to refer to later when the need arises. Whatever you see around yourself leads to the origin of a series of thoughts in your mind. If we look closely at our thinking machinery, thoughts are basically the by-product of the conversion of information (from external sources) to knowledge (about how that information is beneficial to us).

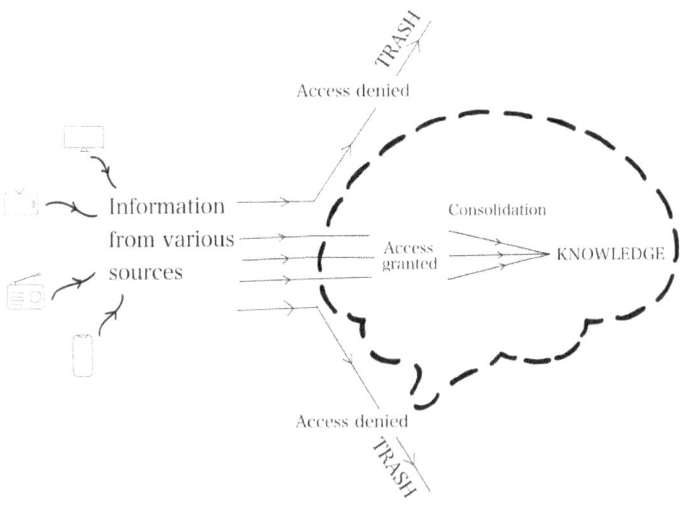

DISRUPTION OF THINKING CYCLES

The speed of thought has been calculated to be about 50 msec. This swiftness of thought is a two-edged sword, that is, the probability of it working in our favour is the same as it working against us. You may wonder where these swift powerful thoughts can go wrong. Well, with the speed! The speed of thought is faster than the speed of light, therefore, the probability of forgetting what you were looking for is greater than a torchlight revealing it in the dark. Research suggests that productive thoughts are powerless when faced with a plethora of distractions waiting to leap towards you.

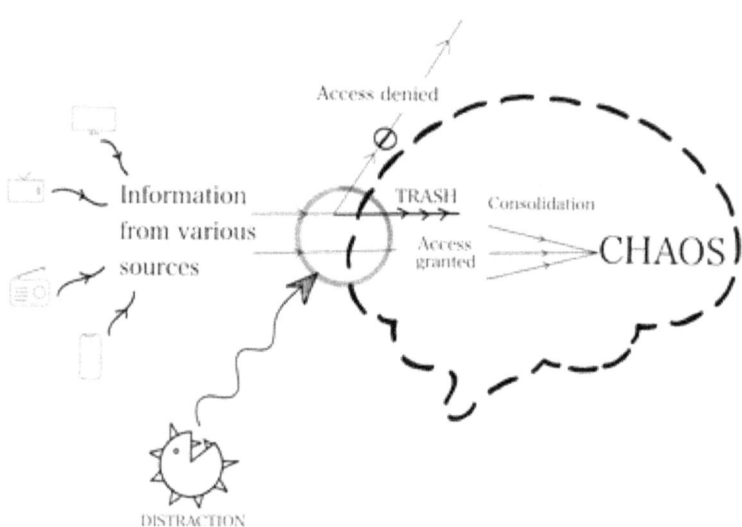

We hardly need research to back that for us as we all understand the power of distraction when for example, you pick up your phone to look up the meaning of a word and conveniently forget all about your intention as you begin sailing in the colourful icons and sumptuous content plated delectably to be devoured. Distraction has this enormous power to always lead us away from the task at hand.

DISTRACTIONS
(Thieves of our consciousness)

One of my friends is a chef and she swears by the power of distraction in food. In her opinion, distractions in food are delicious and addictive and need I say more, In the battle of work versus distractions, the latter always wins unless you've mastered the art of training your mind!! Consequently, humans have not been able to use the concept of neuroplasticity (no matter how old and obvious it may appear now) to our advantage; we rather let it work against us. As discussed earlier, in order to change our brains we need to focus on our thoughts.

Unfortunately, the unwanted information everywhere around us in the form of distraction is also a stimulus that leads to Procrastination of productivity and mental exhaustion.

Recent studies have shown that the percentage of productive time spent on device usage is ever decreasing. Earlier, we used to reach for the phone to carry out an important conversation, now it can be made use of to avoid communication among humans.

<u>THE DISTRACTION KINGDOM</u>

Let us take a look at how the distraction thieves are eating away our precious time: and consciousness

Entertainment

No longer a luxury, the entertainment continues to engulf a major part of our time and attention in today's era. The only small problem with spoiling your brain with a dose of entertainment is that no amount is ever enough. While unregulated entertainment time is directly linked to sleep and behavioural disorders, it is also one of the most potent causes of obesity.

Smartphone

The urge of the millennials and gen z to check their phones first thing in the morning has been magically contagious, and their parents are doing it as well! When you wake up in the morning, there is an urge to check your phone for new messages, notifications, reminders for today, and the latest news. All this is so interesting that we devour this information even without thinking about how these random sources of information are cluttering our brains with collections of individually unrelated yet interesting trivia with questionable authenticity.

What good do you expect your brain to make of it?

PRINCESS AND THE PEA!!
My mentor used to joke about mobile phones becoming the prime cause of sleeplessness among his students. He stated that the "pea" in the "princess and the pea" has been replaced by phones and said that as a result, we have become sleepless, restless, and mindless.

News

The easiest way to get your blood pressure/heart rate soaring at the comfort of your couch at home without even working out!

Social Media

Social media was invented for two important reasons: reaching out and getting in touch. Believe me, none has a clue as to when it got laden with morning coffees and stolen stale quotes that demonstrate self-righteousness. It gradually became a tool to update the world about what you are up to every waking hour.

I wish there was a gauge or a wander meter to measure how easy and attractive has mind wandering become these days. If think you can measure it with your digital usage controls on your gadgets, you're wrong, you seriously have no idea what an hour of deep distraction can do to your focusing muscles.

While also, these days, approval of the world for your actions has become such a potent stimulus to keep going. It not only wreaks havoc on originality and simplicity which every mind is capable of but also on the normalcy of being happy within.

All of the above-mentioned distractions pose one significant threat to your mind. They can put your imagination to rest and make your mind addicted to devouring what they serve.

<u>THE INFORMATION IMPOSTER</u>

An information imposter is a uniquely mischievous member of the distraction family. It leads us to believe we need to swallow it or else we'll miss out on life. This pseudo-knowledge empire encourages distraction addiction! You are so addicted to getting distracted because it comes wrapped up in the guise of quintessential knowledge but once you open the packet, you've gained nothing but lost time!

 You have the urge to check every message that dings your phone because of being addicted to what if? Do you ever face the grave consequences of not watching the next post or reel? No. Don't we need to realize that all thought processes are not useful and all thinking cycles cannot lead to concrete decisions?

We're exhausting our brains for nothing and losing our sleep and peace of mind.

So many thoughts and data transfers are in reality none of our business. We really can be so much more productive by giving up on them. Shifting our consciousness thanks to frequent and often untimely gadget notifications all day takes us nowhere! The junk files take too much of our brain's CPU space, and our mind gets hung when we set out to get creative as it requires focus (and we've lost it conveniently gulping in all that comes our way. Do you know what that costs you? Your originality! Ever heard kids mimicking their favourite cartoon characters? I second that!

<u>IMAGINE A CLEAN BLACKBOARD</u>

With so much to take care of today in the weird wired world, take a moment to think of nothing! When you've been too busy to breathe, take a step back and try to imagine a clean blackboard. If you start by closing your eyes and doing this simple exercise, you'll notice that there is way too much written on the blackboard that you are visualizing even in your imagination. Try to rub those scribbles on your mind's blackboard again and again till you practice getting it squeaky clean. The best time to practice this exercise is before starting your day. Just like having a clean blackboard is important before starting a new class, to have undivided consciousness at the beginning of a new day is priceless!

Untrained consciousness always reminds me of a powerful and apt Shakespearean insult: All eyes and no sight.

TRAINED MIND VERSUS UNTRAINED MIND

"For him who has conquered the mind, the mind is the best of friends; but for one who has failed to do so, his very mind will be the greatest enemy." (Chapter 6, Text 6) Bhagwat Geeta

Indeed, the mind has the remarkable power of self-transformation. When thoughts come to the untrained mind, they often run wild, triggering destructive emotions such as craving and hatred. But practicing mental training, allows us to recognize and control our thoughts and mental episodes as they originate.

An untrained mind needs to unlearn the perennial survival mode! That is our brain trying to trick us into doing the easy work and delaying or cancelling the real work, which leads us to real growth!

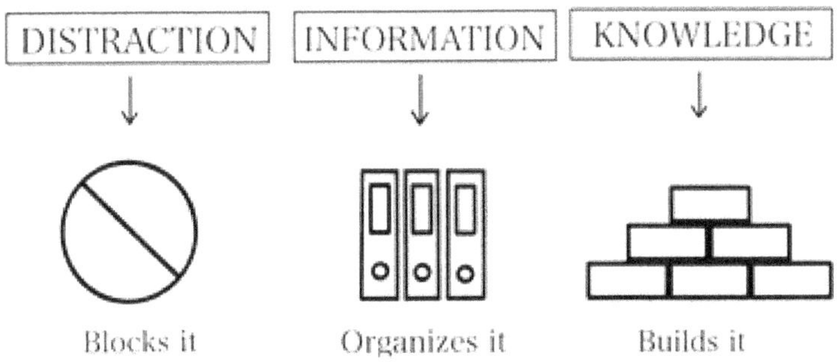

Whenever we think of distractions, information, and knowledge, our brain cannot differentiate the three when left to wander on its own. You have to help it to think clearly and choose what holds value for you in the long run. If you understand how the world inside your head works, the outside world is a cakewalk.

A runner from the team on the verge of winning a relay race accidentally dropped the baton. He felt so ashamed of losing that he hung his head and avoided the team after the race. His teammates went up to him, encircled him, and gave him a group hug! I stood watching from afar and this kind reaction from the team baffled me as much as it did to the discouraged boy. On asking them why they chose to respond in this manner, their moving reply was "we know that he suffered the pain of defeat more than any of us. So, we wanted to stand together as a team."

What a remarkable example of trained minds!!! An untrained mind reacts while a trained mind responds. It made me certain how age doesn't matter in terms of the mind's maturity as seen in these teenagers who had mastered the art of thinking through their thoughts.

Trained minds have a switch-on button, which limits all else going on in the world to reach the brain or the senses.

A lady complained of headaches due to a lack of sleep. I asked her if she'd consulted a doctor, "no, I deleted the games on my phone!!" What an impressive example of a trained mind. Not only did she do what had to be done to take care of what was compromising her sleep, but, she wasn't lost in the excitement to not understand the root cause!

Not everyone has this inbuilt system of recognizing and getting rid of distractions! You can keep practicing to try and reach a state of calm, from where all the chaos around doesn't affect your reason. When struggling to begin treading on this path, why not create a sacred code to remind yourself to focus? If you can't fathom how a code can be powerful enough to drive all distractions away, consider the power of chanting, battle cries, and anthems. These are so powerful because they essentially work on the principle of bringing out the Ekaagra-Chitta (concentrated mind) and narrowing down your consciousness to the objective ahead.

Create your personal mantra

If your brain can be saved from external influences, then it will get back to its extraordinary state, which is how it was created.

<u>THE EXPERIENCE EQUATION</u>

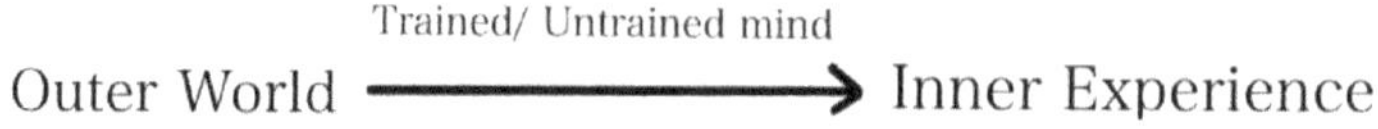

How the outer world translates into our inner experience is governed only by whether our mind is trained or untrained.

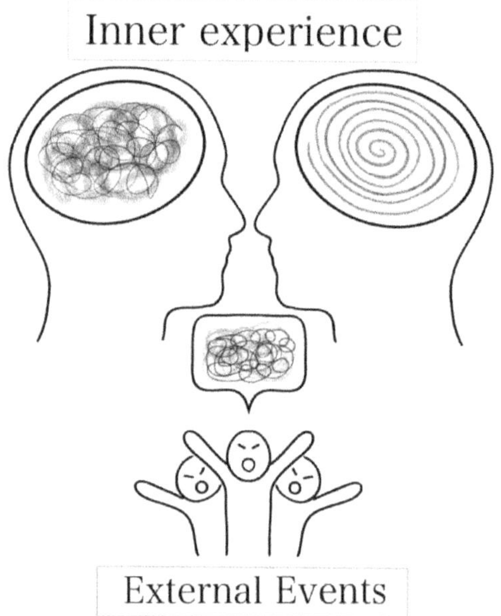

Ever wondered how some beings have used their brains to improve the planet while others struggle to give meaning to their life? Whether it is creating a rocket or a needle, the same brain is at work. Here lies the secret, if the brain can be made to develop the power to ignore external influences, then it can become extraordinary. So that the maximum part of the brain as a CPU is free to do extraordinary work.

Communicate for growth but listen to your inner silence for enlightenment.

It is always easier to provide solutions for others' problems, but when we face them, we fall short of solutions! Just because we are fixing it first-hand, and of course, we are the only ones who will have to face the consequences of our choices!!

Start working on your greatest project: YOU, because you have a bigger purpose in this life, and you need to decipher the signs you have been avoiding forever. While the whole world is busy impressing others, make up your mind to impress yourself.

Your thoughts blossom in the garden of your mind when you water them with deep inner focus, they bloom, and they make you YOU.

"We may work together, live together, come to love or hate each other, and yet our inmost selves forever stand alone. They must live their own lives, think their own thoughts, and arrive at their own destiny."
-George Herbert Betts

Whether we keep finding faults with our brains or embrace our gifts from nature is entirely upon us. The day you understand how you indeed are a product of zillions of years of evolution, you will act like it!

The journey of enlightenment is different for everyone!! Yet we must strive to become our most intelligent and understanding self, intelligent to remain our true self and understanding of the laws of nature that bound us to this earth.

NATURALISM VERSUS NEUTRALISM

Do you think humans evolve over generations? Not quite. Our body evolves every day with old cells dying and new ones being born within us to replace them. Similarly, the human mind opens up to new thoughts and ideas each day to prosper and amend itself to live with the times.

I like to describe the state of being born as a state of Naturalism. It describes how nature created us. Naturalism is the innate ability of a human to respond to the stimuli around it, all favourable and antagonistic. This state is a juvenile state of mind as it keeps busy in recognizing and recording new stimuli surrounding it. It does not know the correct way to process them and respond to them yet.

Once the human mind begins to process the stimuli and its earlier responses as correct or incorrect or unworthy, then it is able to reach a state of neutralism. Neutralism is a state of calm giving rise to no response/reactions to learned and understood stimuli.

Naturalism is adhering to what is expected of a human, whereas, absolute neutralism is expected of sages. Training your mind will take you to the path of neutralism, but staying the same will keep you stuck in the natural and unevolved state. We do not need to be absolute neutralists to be happy. A middle path, such as one designated in Buddhism can serve our purpose of achieving a strong mind.

<u>TAKEAWAY NOTE!</u>

- In the journey of improving yourself, the hardest battle to win is against your pre-programmed mind. Organize your thoughts like you would organize your bookshelf. Always keep your favourites close.

- Not caring what others think is a superpower, not knowing what others think is so important to us, that's why we do know our minds, but we can't know what another person has in mind.

- You need to analyze how exactly the outer world affects you.

- The way in which the outer world translates into our inner experience is governed only by whether our mind is trained or untrained.

- Every brain is extraordinary before it begins to learn the language of distraction and limitation taught by this world

- Our brains cannot distinguish between information and distractions in disguise of information! We need immense training and discipline to develop the skill filter to ignore distraction in the guise of knowledge.

- We all have tiny worlds of our own encased in our very strong skulls and beyond them, let us take very good care of what we feed them with.

- Don't get distracted by what seems necessary or is deemed urgent by others!! Use your brain for your own good.

- If you complain less, you will have less to complain about!

PART II

PART II

4. Understanding your Mind Soil

5. Plough your mind

6. Uproot the weeds

7. Sow the seeds

8. Crop rotation

9. Conserve your mind soil

<u>A LITTLE DISCLAIMER</u>

Before you begin the next section, I urge you to sow a seed and watch it grow!! The following section will be easier to grasp if you witness a growing plant on account of Activity-dependent plasticity which fundamentally means that when you are involved in learning hands-on, your mind registers better and changes for good. You'll observe what your inner self is capable of.

You'll also learn how nature gives way to determination. Sow that seed. Behold the course of nature. You will imbibe how the seed isn't much without the soil (we do need a nurturing environment to reach our maximum potential). And when you're ready, plough your mind.

4.
UNDERSTANDING YOUR MIND SOIL

When we enter this beautiful world, we remain in awe of everything around us. Our senses are open to experiencing the vast magnificence around us. An infant can concentrate on many sounds simultaneously as they take a keen interest in all of them. However, when we grow up, we lose this superpower because we learn that all noises are not worth our attention. The same goes for the ability to see through things (pun intended) which we proudly hail as experience.

While life is happening to us, we tend to toss most experiences as unimportant, let knowledge seep in from some, take a few lessons to heart, and keep growing. We may acknowledge who we are today, but we fail to recall what caused us to become this person. Our experiences get stored in our brains as memories, and they shape who we are. Believe it or not, we are who we are due to the complex hurdles that fall in our way. These hurdles lead to difficult decisions. And making these decisions models who we become, defined by our choices, just like a caterpillar turns into a butterfly. The harsh truth, however, is that not every struggling pupa turns into a butterfly. Some succumb to infections or dehydration too. Similarly, some people get stronger, while others fail to withstand life's stresses. The definition of stress was different for our older generations, it was and is different for us and it will keep changing for the future ones to come. The ever-changing outlook to deal with the freshly defined stresses sums up the beauty of evolution.

The likelihood of whether we will overcome the hurdles or succumb to them lies deeply rooted in the mind. Only if the soil is fertile will it be able to nurture vegetation. Any seasoned gardener starts with understanding the soil type of the garden. This is where you should begin too. Let us start with discovering your mind soil. In this chapter, I will walk you through the systems to gain a better understanding of your mind soil.

<u>DISCOVER YOUR MIND SOIL</u>

The first revelation, and probably the most significant one about your mind is to recognize whether your mind is inherently predisposed to happiness or not. Happiness is one major determinant of a healthy mind which is open to new experiences and has joy seated in its subconscious as a collection of happy thoughts and memories.

To understand how powerful thoughts can be, I want you to do this little exercise. Write down ten words of joy and ten words of sorrow in the table below. It could be objects, people, or places where you experienced the emotions of happiness or sadness.

Joy	Sorrow

You've just created a list of your keys to happiness (to embrace) and your pits of sorrow (to avoid).

Though it is essential to note what brings you joy/sorrow in the above exercise. However, you must also determine to what extent is each pointer bringing you joy and causing you sorrow.

Go back to the list you made and think hard. There could be one point in your joy that cancels/trumps all your sorrows and vice versa. If this holds true, you are beginning to learn more about yourself through this easy exercise.

You will discover what governs your behaviour; seeking joys or fearing sorrows.

Also, you'll discover how your mind weighs both emotions against each other in a particular situation. For example, it could be one phone call from a loved one that makes your day or an angry call from your boss that ruins it. What would you give more power to?

Once you've learned what governs your basic behaviour, you are ready to discover the nature of your mind's soil.

Now that you know what your mind is predisposed to experiencing, here is another simple yet powerful make-believe exercise where you will determine the true elements of your mind's structural framework.

<u>THE MIND-EARTH MODEL</u>

Imagine yourself as an astronaut that has just landed on the planet of your mind. Just like an astronaut looks for signs of life and its

sustainability on a new planet, you are here on a mission to determine if your mind can sustain positive thoughts and is open to new ideas indispensable for a fulfilling life. You have a checklist of the qualities that make a mind habitable to help you evaluate your mind's planet.

Do you see favourable conditions for your dreams to grow and become reality today!! If you want inner peace, your mind should at least be free from clutter, and set aside any negative emotions or memories.

In the course of discovering the mind soil, you get to understand if the soil is fertile enough for good thoughts to be multiplied and good memories to be cherished.

The qualities like the fluidity of water, presence of an atmosphere, presence of gravity, optimum temperature, etc that make a planet habitable, there are prerequisites for a healthy mind too.. and they are compiled as the SCARF rule!

<u>THE SCARF RULE</u>

SCARF is a pneumonic denoting the prerequisites for a habitable mind.

S= STABILITY
C=CONCENTRATION
A=AUTHORITY
R=RECYCLABILITY
F=FLUIDITY

The list of conditions for a habitable mind are:

1. Stability (Balanced extremes)

A state of calm and inward glance is imperative to a balanced mind. A mind's planet should be neither too hot, nor too cold to be habitable. A state of balance and optimum conditions confirms the state of longevity and survival of beings and ideas whether in a planet or a mind respectively.

2. Concentration (Hold the thoughts together)

You've already learned about this quality concerning consciousness and distractions. The innate or learned ability of the mind to be able to focus on the sole objective and determinedly ignore the rest is of utmost importance to be a habitable place. If you do not introspect and learn where your attention is headed, your mind will be in absolute chaos. Keeping a realm of thoughts around your mind that are important to you is just as important as holding the atmospheric layer around a planet.

3. Authority (Recognises its powers)

A mind's ability to retain information and accumulate knowledge is crucial to its survival. Without this gravitational support of memory and intelligence, the necessary information will be of little use to us as we are unable to retain it and make good use of it in the future.

4. Recyclability (Automatically discard unnecessary data)

The constant movement of a planet's crust, air, and water is responsible for carbon recycling and ocean currents. Imagine the power of recyclability you need to have in your mind as it is dealing with thousands of thoughts per day. That's where our memory comes into play. The data that is not considered important by our mind is erased from the memory to free our mind. Retaining useful information is as important as recycling the trash.

5. Fluidity (New interactions)

It refers to the flexibility of the mind and the mobility of its thoughts. Just like the presence of water is the basic need for life and its sustainability on a planet, the fluidity of thoughts is prime for the sustainability of your mind machinery. Fluidity also refers to the dynamic nature of thoughts and ideas. Fluidity in our minds is important to gather new ideas, be creative, imagine new possibilities, and never cease to learn.

Is the soil of your mind fit for ideas to grow and thrive, will good thoughts be multiplied, and good memories be cherished in the present condition of your mind's planet?

<u>SEED VERSUS IDEA</u>

Do you see favourable conditions for your dreams to grow and become a reality today? If you have witnessed a seed growing into a plant, you will be able to correlate it with the birth of an idea in your mind.

How a seed grows? v/s How an idea grows?

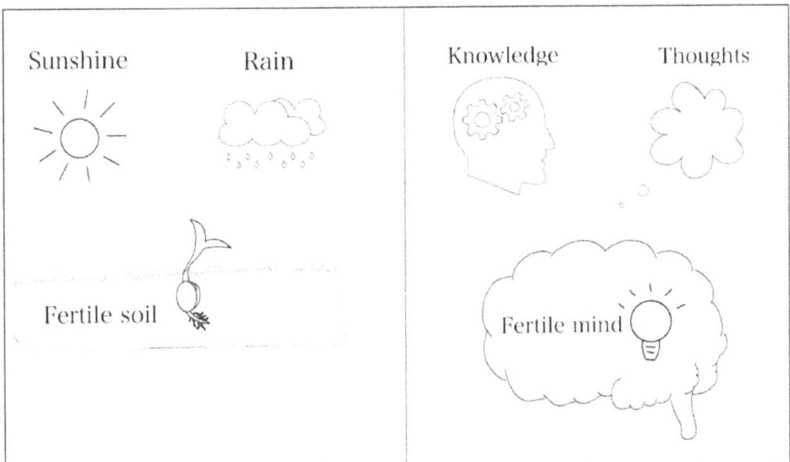

LAYERS OF MIND SOIL

The layers of the mind soil represent the mind's realms in a digestible way to get a clear picture of how our mind works in comparison to the soil.

The mind is divided into three layers for understanding. These layers include,

I.   The Hard Crust

II.   The Middle Layer

III. The Deep Inner Layer

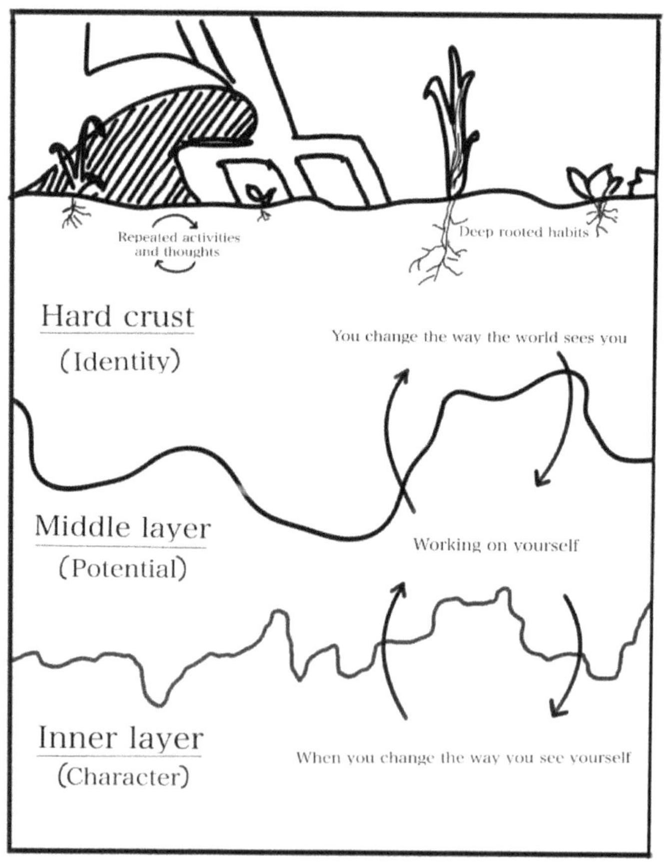

I. Hard Crust

This is the uppermost layer of our mind soil which is formed by the settlement/ sedimentation of thoughts, emotions, and behaviours that have hardened over time.

This layer begins forming after we are born and begin to understand the world and continues to condense with life experiences over time. After a while, these thought patterns get ingrained in our grey matter as the hard crust.

This well-ingrained crust is guarded thoroughly by our subconscious mind in the form of an instruction manual that our mind falls back to when facing survival crises! These form the basis of our lives!

One aspect of the crust is the deep-rooted habits coupled with our daily monotonous routine (only repeated activities, thoughts, and decisions are deep-seated here!). The other aspect is a set of emotional/ behavioural patterns as the conditioned reflexes/ responses we tend to exhibit. It demonstrates how the world sees us and our responses!

This hard crust is accustomed to the daily routine that we have developed and sustained till now! Therefore any tiny change in the quality of sleep, toothpaste flavour, etc is unwelcome and the mind immediately demands tranquillity by heading back to old ways.

This consists of not only the positive habits that work in our favour but also, the negative ones that our minds can mask, e.g. lying unnecessarily, always running late, etc

These are habits/traits that have served us for our lifetime and form the core principles that are time trusted and dependable while maintaining a cordial relationship with the world. These habits have been easy to sustain and live with that we see no point in altering these.

The crust guards our present habits as the skull guards the brain because we have attached our identity to this layer.
It's no wonder that forming new habits and unlearning the old ones is so difficult since it's a battle against our own mind/ inner/ higher self. Whatever name you revere your inner being with.

<u>How can we learn from children?</u>

How can children inspire us? They don't know if they can fail. They only know what learning is. They don't know what failing is. They keep working on it with endless desperation. They don't understand any laws to abide by, so they don't follow any. They are those who do not get discouraged by the constant nagging of how they should/should not follow the rules. They crush the rules and set examples. All of this is possible because children's minds do not have a hard crust.

II. Middle Layer

This layer of the mind soil represents our potential and its nature depends completely on our choices. It shows us how much have we exercised our autonomy for growth.

This layer is of utmost importance because of its versatile nature and for being situated between two dynamic layers. It forms the sole connection between the ingrained hard crust and the 'open to possibilities' deep inner layer.

The outer layer changes with the changes in our environment, and the inner layer changes as we continue to work on ourselves and embrace the new version of ourselves. The middle layer maintains the balance between the two adjacent layers.

This should be the broadest layer in the mind soil which would mean that we are constantly working on ourselves. This layer tends to be the broadest in individuals who consciously choose to leave their comfort zone and is thin to non-existent in individuals glued within the confines of their comfort zone.

III. Deep Inner Layer

This layer represents who we really are, to ourselves. We can be an imposter to ourselves but not this layer, it is the mirror of our shortcomings and our virtues!

This layer is relatively narrow in people pleasers (they always value everyone else above them and have little understanding or regard for their inner selves) as opposed to individuals who have high self-esteem and value their time and purpose on earth.

The only way to reach the deep inner layer is to either break open the upper layers or make them permeable to change.

This is the layer we tend to focus on when on a spiritual path! This is our personality. This is the character we own and are personally aware of. We may or may not be aware of our righteousness, but we do have a bunch of principles that we usually like to stick to. We are exactly how we choose to be, depicted perfectly by this layer. Once our consciousness reaches here and demands a change, we can make amendments to become someone better as the choice always lies with us.

<u>TAKEAWAY NOTE!</u>

- Make efforts to understand what your mind is naturally inclined to feel: joy or sorrow. Once you diagnose the mind soil type, planning therapy becomes easy.

- A habitable mind follows the <u>SCARF</u> rule
    - ✓ STABILITY
    - ✓ CONCENTRATION
    - ✓ AUTHORITY
    - ✓ RECYCLABLE
    - ✓ FLUIDITY

- An idea develops in your mind exactly as a seed grows in the soil. If you don't see favourable conditions for your dreams to grow in your mind, you must make conscious efforts to create them.

- Our mind soil can be divided into three distinct functional layers:
    - ✓ <u>THE HARD CRUST</u> which represents the hardened crust of our external identity
    - ✓ <u>THE MIDDLE LAYER</u> represents the dynamic layers that alter daily in accordance with how we work on ourselves.
    - ✓ <u>THE DEEP INNER LAYER</u> signifies our character and values.

- Any stir of change in one of the layers creates a ripple effect and transforms the rest of the mind soil.

5.

PLOUGH YOUR MIND

Visiting my paternal village since childhood fascinated me. The terrace farming puzzled me so much as to how were the farmers able to get enough yield from very little farmlands. Then a farmer explained their ploughing technique to me and how they took good care of the soil to get a good yield with limited resources. Ploughing is an old practice of overturning the uppermost soil. Much later in life, it struck me as to why can't we plough our minds as we plough our fields. The idea of ploughing the mind intrigued me and I thought that if it works for our fields, why can't we do it for our very own minds? Being from a chief agricultural country like India, I couldn't think of a better example to understand the analogy between ploughing our fields and ploughing our minds. A mind can be just like the field in so many respects.

The idea of ploughing the field is age-old; the concept of ploughing the mind is new, and it works just as well! When we know that the field we are working in is limited, we need to take measures that increase the agricultural efficiency of our fields with a single step of overturning the uppermost soil.

A plough is a farm tool for loosening or turning the soil before sowing seed or planting. Trenches cut by plough are called furrows and represent an analogy to the sulci and gyri (the grooves and bumps) on the surface of the brain. When noticed closely, they look like nature cut trenches to demarcate the various thinking regions!!

Ploughing the field makes us aware of what lies underneath the soil crust and reveals what is buried underneath and plays a key role in governing our crop yield. Similarly, ploughing your mind helps you to think over your thoughts, dissociate yourself from the ego and realize the big picture.

Why are you the best and only person to plough your mind?

Just as getting treated for a skin disease by a neurologist instead of a dermatologist seems bizarre, the responsibility of understanding yourself and your mind's functioning should be undertaken by the one that knows it best. You are the best person to look into the matter when your mind needs help. A tiny nudge of assistance and devotion will make it work much better for you.

When your mind is in question, you are the specialist.

When a child can't find his favourite toy beneath the others, what does he do, he just inverts the toy bucket! A child's toys are tools for him to understand the world simply. Similarly, your thoughts and feelings are tools that help you understand yourself in this quest to have your best life!

During the conversation between Lord Krishna and Arjun at the time of the great battle, Lord Krishna clarified to Arjun the ultimate science of the universe. He revealed the knowledge of the Self to him and bestowed him with the gift of Self Realization.

उद्धरेदात्मनात्मानं नात्मानमवसादयेत्।
आत्मैव ह्यात्मनो बन्धुरात्मैव रिपुरात्मनः ॥

udharet-atmana-atmaanam
na-atmaananam-avsaadyet
aatmaiv hiyatmano bandhuraatmaiv ripuraatmanah

Bhagwat Geeta (Chapter 6, Verse 5)

"One should lift oneself by one's own efforts and should not degrade oneself; for one's own self is one's friend, and one's own self is one's enemy."

Bhagwat Gita states that you are responsible for your own upliftment, and it is your dharma to do so.

<u>THE PLOUGHING REGIME</u>

The process of Ploughing your mind can be systematically categorized as follows:

    a. BREAKING THE HARD CRUST
    b. SHALLOW PLOUGHING
    c. DEEP PLOUGHING

a. Breaking The Hard Crust

In terms of the mind, the hard crust signifies the impenetrable aura of your mind that protects every foreign thought or habit to sneak in and occupy a space in your mind and stir a tsunami of change. You need to make efforts to break this, and to such an extent that you become open to discomfort and vulnerable to change!

The fundamental principle behind breaking the hard crust is to increase the infiltration capacity and permeability of the mind soil which makes it more permeable to let fresh ideas percolate.

When a farmer is ploughing the field, he comes across rocks and stones too. The rocks in the hard crust as hurdles are our friends. Hurdles lead to hard decisions; these tough decisions shape our lives. The easy choices lead us to a vicious cycle of the same tomorrow

I will warn you. This step is going to be the hardest of all! Why? Because your mind has an inbuilt tendency to seek a lifestyle optimal for your survival, however, if you do not change the way you define survival, you may never really evolve! The mind hence, guards our habits, good or bad, our feelings, our limitations, and our shortcomings exceptionally well with the master locker of our brain.

Our survival instinct poses waking up early as a danger and hence the mind tricks you into believing that your body needs more rest to function optimally hence militating against tiny changes that are building blocks to our transformation! This is indeed the toughest conflict to win, the battle with your ever-protective mind! And yes, it takes the maximum amount of force (positive thoughts, constant motivation, and perseverance) to make it happen.

Because our present habits are guarded by the hard crust as the skull guards the brain (the skull here guards the brain against external injury to the same extent as it guards a growing tumour within.

Some examples of breaking the hard crust in your routine life are:
- regulating your sleep cycle/getting up early
- utilizing the coolest feature of your phone- the switch-off button which gives you immense space in life, in case you asked for it lately

- learning something new that you know you will struggle with
- breaking the habits that serve you no purpose.
- creating some form of art every day
- confront the distractions that hinder the formation of new habits
- beat procrastination

If you're up for this, you know it yourself that half the battle is won!
(If you don't believe me, fancy holding a seed in your hand and a spade in another. Once you've dug the soil. How hard is it to sow the seeds?)

Breaking the crust makes the Soil loose for the seeds to be sown easily; similarly, our brains begin to open up to new ideas.
The ploughing process may help you in finding the long-forgotten treasure (talent) or pleasant old memory, which may motivate us for the future.

Don't we often get setbacks in the logical minds because of clouded judgement in the emotional mind? Plough the mind and recognize that these are two separate entities.

So let us plough our minds, one layer at a time.

b. Shallow Ploughing

The act of shallow ploughing is becoming aware of how we are addressing life in real-time. Shallow ploughing refers to what are we doing today to help our present and future selves. Are we heading to improve our potential or lead a balanced life or succumb to the routine of staying the same?

Shallow ploughing aims at making amendments to our choices today, to take a step back and observe what we can do today to enhance our tomorrow.

Shallow ploughing endeavours to upgrade our potential by taking into account three important variables, namely,

- TIME
- ACTION
- GOALS

Think of it like this, at any given time, our actions may or may not be aligned with the goal we are aiming for, or worse still, we may not even be mindful of what our goal is.

The straightforward way to a simplified life is to always know what you want out of your time and plan a sequence of the smallest of actions that are required to be taken for the same.

There's one important reason I am asking you to do this. Ploughing your potential to reveal what you are doing with your time and energy today will give you immense clarity on what step to take next. The most precious blessing to have is the clarity of the path.

There is no one size fits all formula for ploughing as one person needs to work harder than yesterday and the other needs to take a break and ponder upon living. The first step in the ploughing process is to become honest with yourself.

A doctor once told me that she hated going to school. It was only for her father, who kept telling her that she just needed to clear her school, and life was fun after that. Well, she eventually got into medical school, and her dad repeated his lines. She said she couldn't handle the pressure and failed a few exams. Loneliness and depression took over, and she was going to succumb to her failures and drop out, but something magical happened. She heard the same voice from within her. What if she just gathered the courage to get past her present state? What if tomorrow was a brilliant day she had always waited for? She mastered the art of not paying heed to the wild frenzies of her untrained mind and listened to her inner voice. Her dad's constant encouragement had become her inner voice which did not let her fail herself. This little mantra changed the way she looked at life rather than drowning in it.

It is indeed exciting to notice how she kept shallow ploughing till she did change her outlook on life. Her dad had indeed taught her to shallow plough and ingrained courage to face her fears. She dissociated herself from the problem at hand, so she could look for a solution and hence welcome the future with open arms.

Why the earthworms of motivation won't work?

Motivation acts as bouts of enthusiastic energy and drive and it is interesting to note how they are comparable to earthworms while ploughing.

If you've dug the soil during the rainy season, you will notice earthworms and observe how deep into the soil they can go.

The motivation earthworm helps us realize time and again what we are capable of. However, relying on motivation alone will not work, as the dry seasons will make the willpower and earthworms both perish.

c. Deep Ploughing

It is said that the difference between a foolish and a wise man is that a wise man knows he can act foolish sometimes. People who own their ignorance are always successful in the long run. So, OWN YOUR IGNORANCE, own it up, as you would for your achievements.

Deep ploughing is getting to understand who we are to ourselves. It encloses realms of our mind that are truly abstract and known only to us. Our ego, emotional self, our thoughts, our habitual self-talk, and all the traits that define our character.

While the hard crust represents our identity to the world, the deep layer, which is being ploughed in the deep ploughing, represents who we are to ourselves._It implies embracing the definition of ourselves. It is reviving the lost identity, we long to have.

<u>INTROSPECTION: OWN YOUR IGNORANCE</u>

The only way to appreciate the true nature of your consciousness is introspection. Accept it when you feel jealous of someone. Understanding oneself is crucial in overcoming the negative emotions that retard your growth and diminish your liveliness. Plough negative emotions. Judge and improve your behavioural response a lot better after self-realization.

In the process, if you ever reach your brains dump attic, clear it up before the shift in your consciousness to the present moment.

While trying to change a character train in you, it is best to change your definition of yourself in your mind. Stop associating that trait as a part of you. This way it becomes easier for the character to be ingrained. For example, it is always easier to abstain from smoking if you do not associate that with your true character.

Negative emotions such as guilt, regret, hate, anger, and jealousy stop us from thinking AND behaving rationally, and identifying situations from their true perspective. We only tend to see what our mind wants us to and remember what it makes us remember. They are like rust, eat up joy and calm, gradually continuously, and once it tarnishes our mind, there's no returning to the shiny surface ever.

This only prolongs the anger-grief-guilt pathway and prevents us from enjoying life. The longer we let it be, the more it gets ingrained in our minds and, therefore, our identity (the hard crust).

So please unburden yourself of the hidden suppressed emotions that you cannot accept as your own, and try to follow them to their origin. How did you get them inside of you when you weren't born with them? For instance, apologizing for what has been in your mind for ages will make you feel the breeze again. You only feel lighter and open to the positivity around you after you forgive yourself! This life is to be enjoyed, and if you believe in a power that promotes life, you must know that it wants you to be happy!!!

Ploughing deep you will certainly come across lost or forgotten talents.

 I have a personal story to share. My parents noticed my inclination to build jigsaw puzzles at an early age and encouraged me while they believed I was learning something new and keeping busy for hours.

When I was about ten, my cousin came crying over the broken vase she gifted her mom. The vase was enormous, and the wind had caused it to break into over a hundred pieces!!!. I promised to help her as it was a fun activity for me. Being able to help her and make her smile made me happy. Soon it became an everyday affair. I was fixing all broken items at home, in school, and neighbourhood. This alarmed my parents as I usually skipped playing to fix broken items. I was told that I was wasting my time and that all the items I fixed were probably be thrown away later (which was true)! I was convinced that maybe it was all in vain but I couldn't ignore the feeling I had when we finally glued something to near perfection, and the person was thrilled!!

The most fascinating result of the process was, fifteen years down the line, I was joining fractured jaws in surgery! Not that it was impossible without that childhood, but it made things easier for me.

Every skill is precious. Ploughing and hence polishing your early acquired skills makes all the difference.

Let us dig out those lost and forgotten gifts and make full use of them. You really won't know what skill may come in handy much later in life.

Ploughing is not purely about removing all negative emotions and planting positive ones. It is a conscious conversion, where you visualize your mind like a library and arrange the books in order of your preference. Every emotion is pious, to be cherished and protected. You want to keep the testing times close, too, because they made you stronger, just not so close as the times that inspire you to look forward to the future and live the present to the fullest.

It is using all that is registered in your memory for your own good. A person needs to know and realize what they excel at. It is as important as knowing your weaknesses. If you know them and embrace them, you won't ever be weak because of them.

<u>SHALLOW VERSUS DEEP PLOUGHING</u>

Shallow and deep ploughing shape the two major realms of our mind's world. Deep ploughing works on who we are and shallow ploughing works on what we are capable of. Working on these two areas of self-enlargement alternately reduces the burden of our own expectations to overload our brains and lead to quitting.

Shallow and deep ploughing are extremely difficult to isolate as who we are always defined by what we can do and what we do, keeps redefining who we are. E.g. Shallow exercising regularly. Deep would be to discipline your brain to not quit and try harder when you think you are going to give up.

Deep ploughing takes more time and energy, and shallow ploughing improves your life in a short span of time when you diligently practice it.

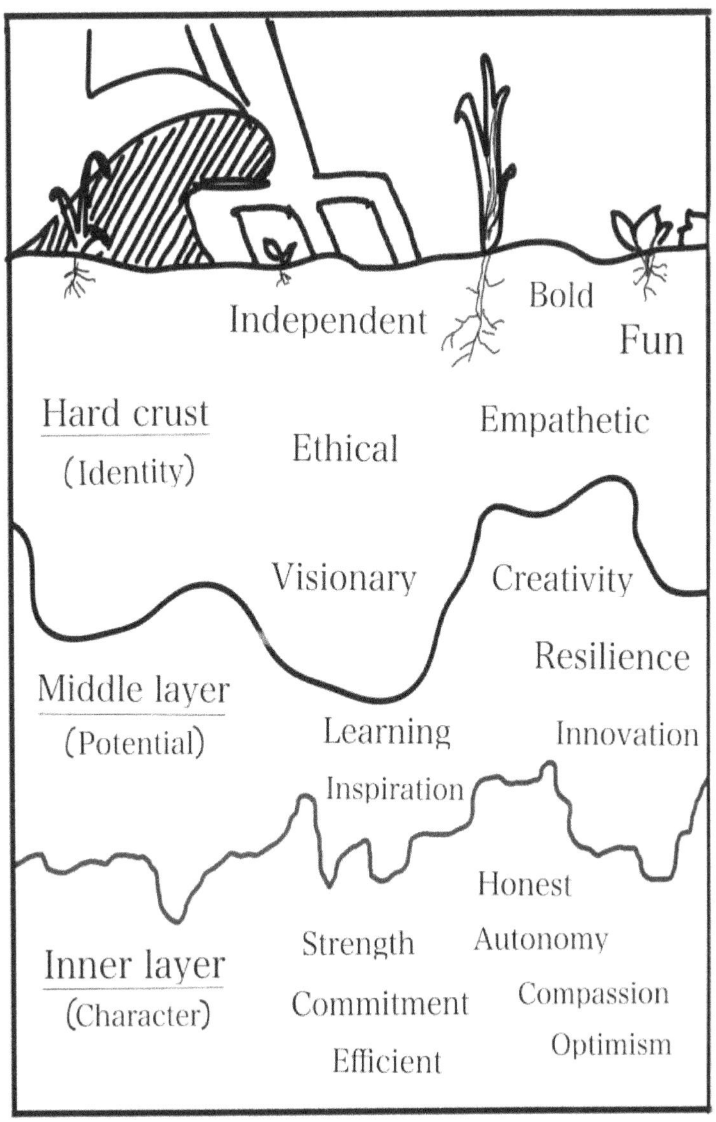
Independent
Bold
Fun
Hard crust
(Identity)
Ethical
Empathetic
Visionary
Creativity
Resilience
Middle layer
(Potential)
Learning
Innovation
Inspiration
Honest
Strength
Autonomy
Inner layer
(Character)
Commitment
Compassion
Optimism
Efficient

<u>BENEFITS OF PLOUGHING</u>

- Ploughing helps you to identify with the functioning of your mind better.

- Plough negative emotions bring them to the surface and deal with them at present

- You will be able to judge and improve your behavioural response a mood a lot better when you know how and what ticks you off

- Your relationships get better because you have clarity about how you want them to be because it is essential for your peaceful existence that your best friend (that's you, by the way) can help and understand you when no one else can.

- The weed roots inhibit crop roots from getting the desired nourishment. The habits we wish to sow are much more fragile as compared to the weeds we constantly nourish. Similar to the disturbing fleeting thoughts or emotions in our mind, they don't bear any fruit but take up the resources (consciousness) of your mind.

- Your mind soil becomes loose for the seeds to be sown easily. Your brain begins to open up for new ideas, new patterns of execution, new habits, and better choices. Basically, breaking the old self-destructive patterns.

Living in Rishikesh for over ten years made me fall in love with white water rafting, but I couldn't bring myself to perform cliff jumping. I had come to terms with the belief that I was incapable of it, and my sane inner voice was protecting me from fear of the unknown and the ability to take up challenges. It made me steer clear of the danger of a bad fall and the magic of a life-changing confidence-boosting experience simultaneously, and it wasn't like I ever dreamt of performing it. I just knew I couldn't do it because I needed to be safe. One fine day, I was a part of a group of fourteen friends that decided to perform cliff jumping one after the other. I still remember telling myself that I had lost my mind to have agreed to participate in the ritual. We lined up and jumped. It was a fall, a conscious decision at that, to jump from a cliff 50 ft high and fall in ice-cold Ganga and hurry back to the bank without knowing how to swim.

When I recall that moment today, it sends shivers down my spine. It was much more than a cliff jump. It fed my soul. I can still feel what I experienced at that moment. My body felt weightless and my spirit free. I'd broken the crust while up in the air when gravity took its course, and my fears evaporated!

This experience brought me the strength I had never known before. I was fascinated to learn to swim, which I did, the following year. Now all this might seem too small victories to share, but if you trust the process, you'll know how engaging and rewarding these victories against your old self are. The endorphin release is way beyond what chocolate has to offer!

The prime purpose of ploughing is to turn over the uppermost soil, bringing fresh nutrients to the surface while burying weeds and crop remains to decay. Imagine doing this to your cluttered brain, combing the sulci and gyri and trashing the load of unnecessary information which is bombarded upon by the distraction devices we feed it with all day.

I am not going to teach you about your goals here. Who can know your personal goals better than you? I am just trying to make your mind simpler for you to understand and utilize to the fullest.

Plough your mind so that you know:
- WHAT TO EXPECT?
- WHAT TO EXPEL?
- WHAT TO ACCEPT?
- WHAT TO NURTURE?
- WHAT TO TREASURE?
- AND HOW OUR MINDS CREATE THE FUTURE!

Ploughing the mind signifies the inherent tendency of humans to improve with time and reach for excellence. We wouldn't trade this quality for anything. The most difficult part is the beginning. A marathon seems tough only when you cannot visualize the finish line. Your mind has a habit of tricking you and telling you it's okay even if you don't try, but friend, you won't know what you can do unless you try.

Our constant urge to improvise

When we created the wheel, then the cart, then the cycle, the motorcycle, cars, and even airplanes. We don't stop anywhere. We couldn't satisfy our curiosity and imagination, and there was always a "what next?" And the human brain always replies with a "why not?"

It takes humans at least three decades to get feedback on whether evolution worked its way for us in the next generation.

Ploughing in the simplest terms means that you're not letting the mind soil stay stagnant. It is turning over the soil to come up with solutions to long-term problems that we designate as "normal" life and do nothing about them. Plough your mind, rotate the nourished soil of your brain that holds your thoughts together!

Alternate shallow and deep ploughing

Work on your identity, your abilities, and your character alternately rather than doing all the work at once. When you have a plan, you can pay heed to all the aspects of your being that determine your true nature.

When a field is ploughed, the worms and insects near the roots of the crops are brought to the surface in the process and eaten up by birds.
If you notice, just by ploughing over and acknowledging the traits that don't serve you, you can pay close attention to their source and get rid of them!

Ploughing the mind not only increases your productivity but also leads to inner peace, helps in sleep disorders, mental block relief, success, long and disease-free life. We want to keep combing the brain to get rid of what doesn't belong here and cherish what was imbibed by it in developing into what it is today!

Plough every season

Our professor once exclaimed "Baba Black Sheep…" in an interrogative tone and we instantly replied with "have you any wool?" He was thrilled at our response and went on to explain to us how repetition is the key to excel, even in memorizing something. He said that when you learnt this poem for life, you didn't understand what it meant.
Plough your mind. You'll be surprised with the yield!!

<u>TAKEAWAY NOTE!</u>

When it comes to ploughing your mind, you are the specialist.

Ploughing your mind is done in three steps:

1. <u>Breaking the hard crust</u> which involves being open to challenges and vulnerable to change. This is the most uncomfortable part of the process as it changes your routine.
2. <u>Shallow ploughing</u> involves improving what you are capable of. It is putting conscious efforts into making the most of your time, energy, and consciousness.
3. <u>Deep ploughing</u> is the act of changing the world within you to understand yourself and become a better version of yourself.

Motivation is like earthworms, it is helpful for a head start but its inspiration is limited to favourable seasons.

YOUR CUSTOM PLOUGHING PLAN

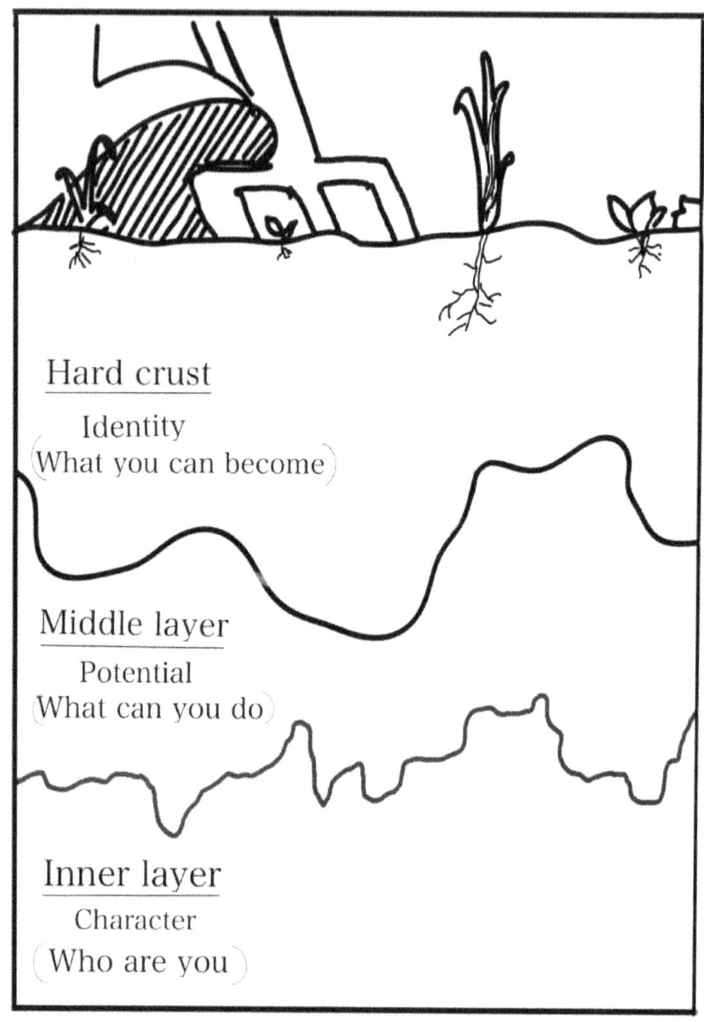

6.
UPROOT THE WEEDS

Have you realized while taking care of a plant that though the fertilizers have to be planned and replenished for the plant to thrive, but, from nowhere, weeds like grasses appear and start growing in the pot, without any invitation, just like that?

The same goes for our minds, good thoughts and habits will need much contemplation to reside, but unwise thoughts will just come up from nowhere and lodge themselves deeply in our minds.

In this chapter, we will recognize the mental weeds instilled deep in our minds, trace their origin and uproot them for good.

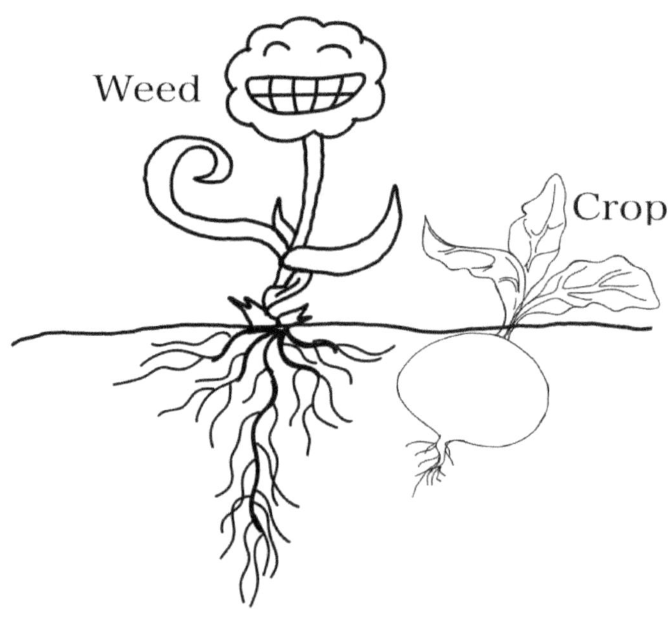

Just like a weed has stronger and deeper roots as compared to a crop, our mental weeds are also deeply ingrained in our minds. The weeds have stronger and deeper roots as compared to the desired crops (laws of nature, fatefully) we want to yield consciously. These roots strangle the roots of our intentional thoughts and cause them to perish.

It is vital to consciously abandon the thoughts and emotions that don't resonate with you, in order to become your best self. Remove the unimportant unserviceable weeds which are thriving on the nourishment of your consciousness.

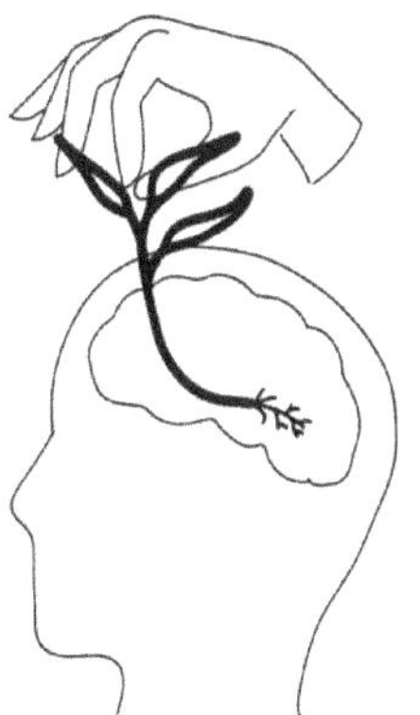

When people will not
weed their minds,
they are apt to overrun
with nettles.

Horace Walpole

Do you often give up on trying new things? Because you think you can't learn/unlearn old patterns? Our brains have experiences stored in the form of memories that shape who we are. Though all hands are created equal, it's the minds that perceive, learn and develop the artistry we idolize and admire!

What is it that holds you back? It is you.

You program your shortcomings. You feed your failures. You are the one actively creating hurdles in your mind; nature never created any.

<u>MENTAL WEEDS</u>

Let me bring your attention to the most damaging mental weeds to the human thinking machinery which also harm the physical body in the long run!

When you plough your mind and remove the unserviceable weeds, you come across the dormant seeds of our unique talents and sow and further nourish them. That is our true path.

Here is a list of the most damaging mental weeds. Feel free to extend the list and add more for a customized list that works for you. It is important to name them, track them to their origin and uproot them.

   a. Fear
   b. Self-doubt
   c. Learned helplessness
   d. Negativity bias
   e. Stress
   f. Procrastination
   g. Negative reminders

a.Fear

Researchers are of the opinion that we are born with only two kinds of fear: the fear of falls and the fear of loud sounds. All of the other fears except these two (which ensure survival) are the fears we take up while growing up, usually instilled by listening to the experiences of fellow humans.

Fearing things we haven't known much about makes us

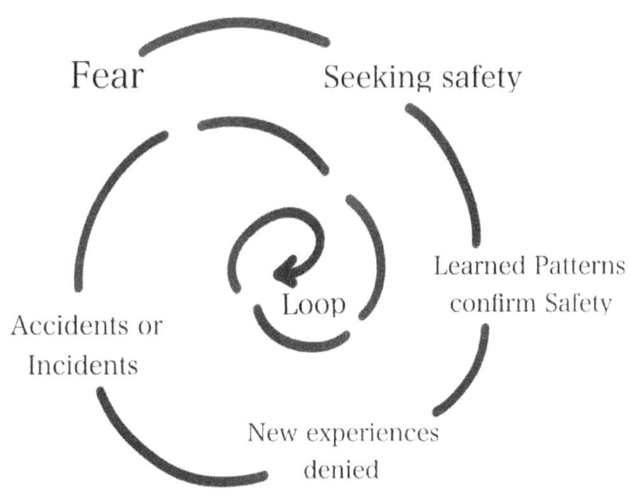

The Fear Loop

habitual to always fear the future or a situation in the future that we are not well informed about. Before we know it, a vaccine, a jungle safari, and an insect have all become too scary for us to handle.

Have you ever confronted fear on purpose?

Try it sometime. It is extremely empowering to do something uncomfortable. I am not asking you to go too far. You can start by taking a cold shower and observe how your body while getting used to it, no more flinches when the cold water hits it. Overcoming tiny fears makes you believe in yourself to do more powerful things that you are capable of. Rather than drowning in the vicious loop of fear, embrace your horrors and conquer them.

b.Self-doubt

Self-doubt, unlike fear, is always introduced to you by worldly beings. We don't have it from the beginning because we don't need it to live. What we need to live is there is us. And self-doubt has no place inside of us.

You had no machine fitted into you which constantly doubts your behaviour. You were programmed to be curious and inquisitive to learn and improve. You did not know how to judge yourselves harshly till others showed you how it's done.

When you doubt yourself, what you're essentially doing is barring yourself from the magnificence within you. A more serious consequence is that it ultimately leads us to believe in ourselves only when someone from the outside world validates us, and this goes on until we no longer feel fulfilled or complete within. We crave appreciation as if our life depended on it.

Self-doubts are like preinstalled gadget apps that are of no use to you, yet drain the device of ram and don't let your mind think clearly and efficiently.

In all sanity, self-doubt leads to self-destruction. Uproot this weed before it eats you up inside.

What you say to others may matter sometimes, but what you say to yourself matters a great deal, always.

c. Learned helplessness

This one is my favourite because of the utterly complex way in which it functions. Most of us are so involved in our suffering that we fail to see the big picture. Learned helplessness can be categorized as a type of self-doubt, but a very complex one.

Have you ever heard people say to you, that they are in trouble, but they cannot do anything about it? That's what learned helplessness is all about. Just because our efforts didn't solve a problem dozens of times in the past, we accept it to be our fate and believe the lie that no matter what we do to solve it, nothing will change.

To understand this weed simply, take the example of a baby elephant. A little elephant is tied with the help of a rope just enough to hold him. He tries a lot to break free but fails. This failure gets so deeply ingrained in his thinking machinery that he believes that he will never be able to break free. This leads him as an adult elephant to not even try and free himself from the bondage. The elephant stops putting in any effort to solve the problem at hand because he has been subjected to countless efforts in vain and believes that he is helpless in this regard.

We simulate this behaviour too often to ignore it. When an effort doesn't work, we stop putting in any effort when encountering a similar hurdle.

Just because you failed several times in the past, it makes you trust with certainty that no matter how much you try, you can do nothing to change the outcome, so why even try?

The only way to unlearn something is to break the mundane patterns which make their way deep into your mind. In the context of learned helplessness, it is important to remind yourself that there's always a way around a problem. You just haven't been able to figure it out yet. Keep trying with the older methods as well. They will work. Something will work.

<u>d.Negativity bias</u>

A perfect holiday can be stored as a bitter memory if you lose your phone while returning. Studies have shown that negative influences affect us far more than positive ones and we tend to remember and recall them for longer. Our brain plays a very crucial part here.

It's hard to argue that negativity bias doesn't serve any meaningful purpose in our lives. Negativity bias is an inherent tendency to help us avoid potentially harmful stimuli we are unaware of such as being scared of snakes as they could be venomous. But, as we grow old this hardwired tendency is not as useful as it once was. Brain waves tend to travel the shortest path. By shortest path here I mean the 'easy old ways' path. Our brains get used to consistently seeking the most unpleasant part of an otherwise fantastic experience. What is important for survival becomes a problem when We begin to look for problems in the solutions.

Match the following shapes to the names of the animals they represent.

Rat   Fesh   Frog

Before you begin this exercise, if you spot the spelling error, this signifies an innate inclination to negativity bias towards wrong spellings.

Scrutinizing the world through the lens of negativity bias is a sure-shot recipe for trouble! this is frequently a precursor of overthinking and revisiting the past for clues to support your present judgement. All ado about nothing!

e.Stress

The early man dealt with the stress caused by a predator by running away. Expending that stress in the form of running away relieved it. We cannot do that to so many frightening stressful situations today, which leads to compounded resentment towards ourselves in the long run, which in fancy terms is stress.

One astounding truth about stress is: You've nurtured its growth! Stress is like a hung file in our mind which gets played over and over again. Ignoring the built-up inside you is like ignoring the most primitive need, i.e. the response of fight, flight, or fright when a stressful situation arises. One must always find ways to beat the stress caused by mundane life on a regular basis with the help of exercise and meditation.

f.Procrastination

I remember an acquaintance who was fondly called Arya Stark in the friends' group. Not knowing the origin of her nickname, I imagined her to be fierce and courageous. It was only after a few months that I got to know that she loved procrastination so much that she'd say "not today" to almost everything. The naming now appeared intelligent and hilarious at the same time!

Do you procrastinate just for the heck of it? Would you rather play a game than get that damn project done or learn a new skill because anything unproductive is more fun and more fun is what the brain is always seeking?

Life is not any longer than a few thousand weeks and there's certainly not much time to postpone living for later. Weed out delaying as a habit and make your days more purposeful.

g.Negative reminders

On the day of academic results, Soham would attend his children's parent-teacher meeting, collect their grade card and lock it away. This was his way of him showing kids that their scores didn't prove their worth. He was certainly not having these negative reminders around to set limitations on the kids. What happened in the past will change, you need to give it away to make way for the future.

Contemplate the number of negative reminders around you. Negative reminders could be a regular item such as a pen, table, or toy. It is only you who knows the story behind it and the power it holds to elicit negative feelings in you.

We want to crush the old, hurtful neurological pathways in the brain and memory! No more tension headaches, anorexia, or reliving them.
Remove the negative reminders around you. They send a feedback mechanism to your mind to never escape the vicious circle of melancholy. Negative reminders are a greater cause of stress than the self as they don't allow you to think beyond your past.

THE WEED WEB

Interrelation Among Mental Weeds

The chart above represents the level of correlation among the mental weeds at large. Each of the mental weeds is not only occupying the healthy mental space otherwise designated for our future forward thoughts, but also nurturing and strengthening other weeds.

As an example, imagine that you are scared of public speaking but have great ideas to share. The fear of the new experience will lead to doubting yourself and your ideas. You will start questioning yourself if your ideas are actually good enough to be shared. Even the thought of standing up and talking to people will cause stress and anxiety in you and if you still overcome all these and finally try one day, your talk may or may not be how you had imagined it to be. A simple failure leads to more stress, learned helplessness, and eventually procrastination. Worst still, if you have a reminder of the day your public speaking didn't go as desired, you'll be forever stuck in the thought of not even trying again. That is how strongly these weeds support each other.

The arrows in the weed web represent the affiliation between two weeds. A double-headed arrow denotes that these weeds lead to each other's growth whereas a single-headed arrow represents that one weed as the origin and the other as the consequence and the reverse is not true.

Looking closely, you will notice that negative reminders around us are the only weeds that can be recognized and uprooted once and for all. They nurture other weeds but other weeds don't lead to them.

After narrowing down your mental weeds, all you need to calculate is how much mental force is required to uproot a habit, a negative thought, or an emotion. Uproot those weeds before you begin your new journey to become a better person or maybe a new person with a plain blackboard brain. The idea is not to do a factory reset, it is to eliminate the bugs while keeping the files you need.

The roots of these uprooted weeds act as humus when left to rot, just like the old negative thoughts will be destructed or questioned by your mind's reasoning. This will lead to a better understanding of your thinking patterns which pave the way for clear thinking, knowing the good from the bad, the necessary from the rubbish.

<u>TAKEAWAY NOTE!</u>

- You are the one actively creating hurdles in your mind; nature never created any.
- A mental weed has stronger and deeper roots and is well ingrained in your mind. It takes a lot of mental force and practice to get rid of these weeds.
- Identify and remove all the negative reminders from your environment which make you believe that you cannot work past your present circumstances.
- Make a list of the mental weeds you want to uproot and analyze the connection between them. There is always a pattern these weeds create you coexist in your mind.

7.
SOW YOUR SEEDS

I precisely remember getting my first bicycle and my parents not letting me ride alone. I kept asking my dad when will he let me ride it alone without him watching over me. He said, "when you're a big girl", I asked when I will be a big girl. Then he said, "when you are capable of picking yourself up and reminding yourself to start afresh, you'll be a big girl when you remember to repeat these to yourself even when I am not there next to you."

During my childhood, I learnt something fascinating. I could talk to myself like how ma papa spoke to me as if I were two persons at the same time, the one who said and the one who listened. This power does come in handy when you have to continue adulting your brain, your entire life.

All the exercises of determining the mind soil and pulling out the weeds bring us to the most evident part of the ploughing journey: sowing the seeds.

Self-awareness is the first seed to sow. If you don't know where you are, how will you know the route to your purpose?
It is only after you achieve peace of mind by ploughing your mind, will you know what seeds you want to sow. The buzz won't affect you; the trends won't distract you; other versions of you won't restrain you.

<u>SELF-AWARENESS</u>

Self-awareness is a strong precursor to self-love because love is not only about being critical of oneself but also about appreciating all that you are made up of; good or bad.

Mental seeds are sown to yield a thought process, a solution, a habit, or a behaviour. We are consciously or otherwise, constantly doing so with the simple act of making choices every day. What gets nurtured in the mind, stays rooted and what gets abandoned dies down.

<u>TYPES OF MENTAL SEEDS</u>

Seeds are of two types:

1. Dormant seeds within your mind soil
   Just activate and nurture them. Look for the dormant seeds of brilliant talents unique to you. Sow then again and nourish them

2. Seeds that consciously sow to help make your life better. e.g. seeds of compassion, perspective, etc.

As you sow, so shall you reap, only if you plough it right and plough it often.

We may sow the same seeds (thoughts in mind but how well it develops into a seedling. It depends so much on how the idea was playing around in the brain. That's what ploughing does. It sends your perfect idea/thought to the thinking machinery and produces a feedback mechanism.

There is always a perfect season to sow the seeds. The intelligent farmer waits for it and then gives his best shot at cultivation. Remember, these seeds will grow into strong plants and then strong trees if you nurture them constantly. Take care of them and water them often. Make sure some sunshine of your consciousness regularly reaches your orchard and enjoy the fruit of inner joy.

SOWING THE SEEDS

Choosing your seeds is entirely up to you. I am not here to help you choose your seeds, I can just let you know which ones to grow together to have a fulfilling yield. The next chapter will cover the set of seeds to be sown together to help you gain more from the fields of your thoughts. Just before we move ahead, some ways of taking care of seeds are:

- Trust the process and take the leap without prior expectations or judgement. All those who have ever been able to reap benefits from sowing positive habits were the ones who didn't expect quick miracles but were ready for the long haul.

- Create space for the new seeds to be sown. This is not possible unless you devote time, and energy and arrange prominent reminders around you.

- Always place more seeds than the plants you need. Allow them to grow beyond time and judgement as not all of them will grow at the pace you intend them to.

8.
CROP ROTATION

"If you want to have clean ideas, change them as often as your shirt."
Francis Picabia

Our farmers keep changing the crops that they grow every year and at every cycle because they know from experience that sowing the same crop over and over again will lead to reduced fertility of the soil. In a similar fashion, we can learn from their experience and discover a unique combination of different crops to sow in our minds so that the fertility of our mind soil is replenished in the course of reaping the maximum benefits. Crop rotation in the context of the mind refers to changing the seeds (in the form of ideas) to be sown so that all of the brain areas are working and active. Why do you gravitate toward certain activities and not others? Look within. This can help you gain a deeper understanding of yourself and what makes you tick.

For example, You may be a great writer or mathematician, but you might have to create art to activate all regions of your brain. Learning with left and right brains and training the two together can increase your output manifolds. e.g. how does writing or plating with your non-dominant hand makes changes in your brain?

We believe that we can't paint because somewhere, we have compared our work with someone else's perception of perfection, and stopped playing with colours.   Adult brains function differently compared to children. Children are more open to new experiences unless fear has been fed to them, but adults try to pass over new and previously uncomfortable experiences.

Planting new and uncomfortable crops make us open to unexpected yields. If you've always thought of yourself as a "numbers person" or a "creative one", the endeavour should be to reach the zones of our mind we didn't know we possessed. Renew your energy and focus. Break your established mould and wander outside of your comfort zone. Taking a new route to an identified destination, immersing yourself in foreign art, taking a course in a subject you find exciting and daunting at the same time, etc can lead you to a change you'd never imagined. We need to let the light of consciousness enter the depths of our mind's ocean and see what treasure lies there.

<u>MIND CROPS</u>

Mind crops can be largely divided into these three categories:
1. Creative
2. Intellectual
3. Social

You may not truly fall into any of these, but you can play to your strengths and continue broadening your mental horizons. A normal, healthy brain is capable of lifelong learning and boundless creativity.

However, these categories are definitely not rigid. for example, a creative person can find it easy to solve intellectual problems by thinking outside the box, learning a new language is getting creative, requires intellect, and undeniably pushes you to be social to exercise it.

In the following descriptions, lie ideas to enhance your mental crop yield. You can sow some creative, intellectual, or social seeds in your mind by following one or more of these ideas.

<u>CREATIVE</u>

- Learning to draw your imagination into paper.

- Learn to play a musical instrument.

- When you get new ideas, write them down and work on developing them further.

- When solving a problem, try to brainstorm and create multiple ways to solve it.

- Pay heed to nature and its ways, a new leaf unfolding, an insect at work, cloud patterns, etc.

- While relaxing leave the TV off and let your mind be present with you.

- Read about and listen to the creative ideas of others. You might discover the seed of an idea you can grow or set your imagination free.

<u>INTELLECTUAL</u>

- Spending time reading your favourite book and then writing about how you liked it.

- Being curious and acquiring knowledge about everything unfamiliar to you like cars, genetics, food science, etc

- Learning new synonyms for fresh vocabulary.

- Playing crossword and sudoku puzzles.

- Play memory or board games

- Take on a new hobby that requires you to focus.

- Conducting elaborate research to answer a question.

<u>SOCIAL</u>

- Improving your public speaking skills.

- Striking a conversation with strangers. This one will especially be a hint of fresh breeze.

- Learning about and respecting other people and their culture.

- Doing group projects both as a leader and a participant.
- Learning the art of getting a message across via storytelling.

- Sharing your knowledge with a group of amateurs.

- Understanding and empathizing with children's lives and difficulties.

THE CROP ROTATION WHEEL

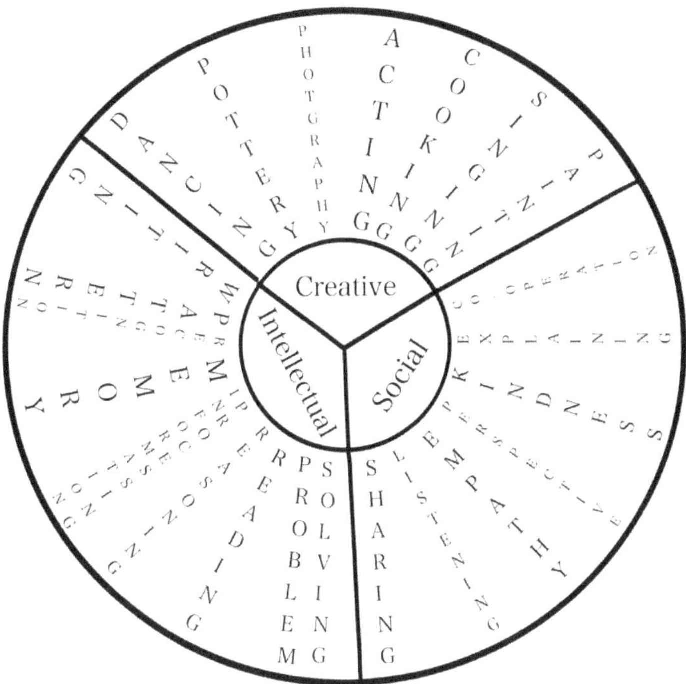

The above wheel is a representation of seeds to sow. Feel free to get inspired and create your customized crop rotation wheel.

REST AND RECOVERY

When we focus on how much is left to be done, we tend to overload our expectations and shoulders in the name of productivity. Seeds take time to grow. The bottom line is to not get so engrossed in the process of acquiring knowledge that you forget to give your brain a break. The first time blocks you assign to your calendar should be for doing nothing as that's also really important to begin again with double force after a recovery.

<u>TAKEAWAY NOTE!</u>

- Create your personal crop rotation wheel and see how many crops you can sow in a week, a month, and a year!

- Pick out one crop from each of the groups and try to better yourself at them for a month. You will be surprised at how easily it becomes a part of your personality.

- Do one thing that challenges you every day. Your brain gets used to accepting change and failure as a part of learning.

- Refrain from doing similar activities for long hours, your mind needs a break just like you do else it goes into a state of burnout

- Block out your calendar for "no activity" time. Do nothing and just let your mind wander.

9.
CONSERVE YOUR MIND SOIL

This is one special revelation for all those who have come this far and experienced this journey of self-discovery paralleling a seed, a seedling, a plant, and a tree. The popular belief stating that the more we use our brain, the better we become, is only partly true. It is prudent to understand that the more you use your brain for sharpening your skills and getting better results works in your favour but using it to the level that it gets exhausted and passes into a state of burnout does the opposite. Although the possibilities for growing vegetation on this planet are unlimited, the soil we have to nurture its growth and hold its roots is limited. We need to conserve our mind soil as the ideas and ability of the mind is unlimited but the ground used to make them grow and thrive is limited.

But how can one conserve the mind soil?

The answer to this question was accidentally given to me as a sermon by my art teacher.

When I was twelve, one day my art teacher asked me what I considered the most difficult aspect of free art. I told her that for me it was to paint a fine line with a brush as I was still learning to practice strokes and take good care of my brushes. She promised to help me and stated that once I learn the technique, I will be able to paint fine lines even with the thickest of brushes.

The next day, as she demonstrated painting fine lines, she kept hinting that if one gathers all of their focus, everything gets easier. While I was trying to understand what she meant by that, she made me practice for an entire session of two hours, and in the end, finally, I could do it.

Now that I was getting better at it, she asked me what was different this time. "I focussed", I said, "...and forgot everything else." She claimed that I forgot something important which puzzled me. I didn't understand. She said, "You forgot to breathe. That is what creates undeterred focus. When you hold your breath to focus, you can't go wrong." I instantly realized that I did hold my breath every time I painted a fine line.

LESSON 1: HYPER FOCUS is the key to doing what you think is difficult.

The next day, she asked me to practice painting the trunk of a tree and dispensed some lemon yellow paint on the palette. I found it funny, to begin with, a colour that doesn't belong to the tree trunk and debated that. The deep brown will eventually mask the lighter yellow anyway. But she explained. That's now how you should see it. Nature has layers, and so should your art. If you want to depict nature. You need to identify and appreciate the layers. A tree trunk is not just the bark; it's the centre also that accounts for the colours of the trunk from the outside. It was so deep an explanation that it stuck with me. The final painting brought so much more happiness because it was so LIFE-LIKE. It looked more similar to how nature created it. I had understood the layers and wondered if that's how art brings us close to ourselves. Eager to learn more I asked her what was the most difficult part of art in her opinion.

Lesson 2: Your true nature is the consolidation of layers. No single layer alone can define your identity or character.

She offered to show me one of her works to explain it. She pointed toward a spectacular painting of Lord Krishna and said that the most difficult part was to paint the white garland worn by Lord Krishna. When asked why. She said The most difficult part of art is to create magic by blending colours but maintaining the purity of white. White is the most difficult colour to use since other colours easily mix with it to make it impure. This is something that stuck with me. The same goes for our ever-vigilant minds; it is challenging to keep them stable and safe from external influences.

Lesson 3: It is easier to blend yourself with the surroundings but extremely difficult to maintain the purity of your mind. Don't mingle with people you don't wish to be like, or else, your personality will change its colour.

On the last day of classes, she showed me all her paintings and announced that they were up for sale. I became sad and thought that she didn't love her creations enough to hold onto them. She sensed the disappointment in my expression so I gathered the courage to ask her how she could part with them in exchange for money. She replied I want to share my happiness with others in the form of art. My entire garage is full of paintings. I want blank canvases to replace them and inspire me to create fresh art.

That was the day I learnt how someone could give away their creation to the world to celebrate in exchange for a clean slate to start afresh!!

Lesson 4: Share your talent with the world to celebrate and create a fresh mindset to start over new.

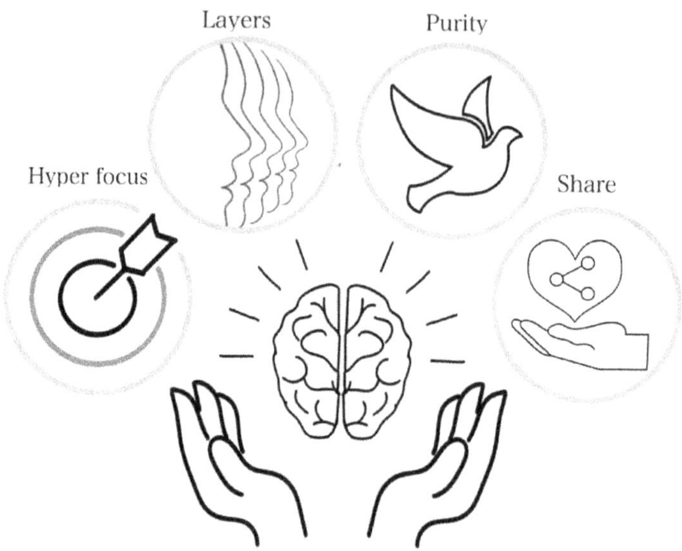

You can plough your mind all you want to reveal gems and get rid of your weeds, but, do remember to conserve your soil in the process. That's the only place where your ideas grow and thrive.

Your potential is immeasurably more than you have ever been authorized to believe

Therefore, whenever you talk to yourself, talk highly of yourself. Remember, becoming like someone else is such an underestimation of your true calibre. Conserve your minerals. In this age of trends, find your true calling and stay unique.

I wish you smooth sailing on your journey from naturalism to neutralism. Plant more trees (thoughts/ ideas). If you do not choose the roots (ideas) with which to hold your soil, your brilliant mind and consciousness will be worn away with the routine life. Distractions may come from the outside, but transformation always comes from within! Because moulting is not just opening the wings, it's also about leaving the chrysalis.

WE AND THE BOOKS HAVE SPINES IN COMMON

KEEP READING, KEEP STRETCHING